THE RULE OF SAINT BENEDICT

LATIN & ENGLISH

Translated by

LUKE DYSINGER O.S.B.

SOURCE BOOKS
TRABUCO CANYON CALIFORNIA

This papercover edition first published in 1997

Library of Congress Cataloging-in-Publication Data:

Benedict, Saint, Abbot of Monte Cassino.
     [Regula. English & Latin]
     The rule of St. Benedict : Latin and English / translated by Luke Dysinger.
          p. cm.
     Includes bibliographical references and index.
     ISBN 0-940147-27-0 (pbk.)
     1. Benedictines--Rules. 2. Monasticism and religious orders--Rules. I. Dysinger, Luke, 1953– . II. Title.
BX3004.A21997
255' . 106--dc21   96-37933
                                          CIP

ISBN 0-940147-27-0

Published by:
SOURCE BOOKS
Box 794 Trabuco Canyon
CA 92678 USA

Printed and bound by KNI Inc. Anaheim, California

To my parents, Glen and Christine Dysinger,
who taught me to love the printed and spoken Word.

INTRODUCTION

The Rule of St. Benedict has shaped Christian understandings of community and the practice of Christian prayer for almost 1500 years. For all that time it has been read, meditated upon, interpreted, modified and—most important of all—lived. When in the early middle ages Christian monks were commissioned to preach the gospel to both pagans who had never heard it, and to lapsed Christians who had turned back to paganism, it was the Rule of St. Benedict that shaped the communities they formed and the way of prayer they taught.

The Christian Church today faces a challenge very similar to that faced by monastic missionaries more than a millennium ago. The pull of what might be called 'pragmatic despair' is as powerful today as it was in the time of St. Augustine of Canterbury and St. Boniface. They faced a resurgence of paganism; we experience a resurgence of agnosticism, atheism, and anti–religious hostility. The root of the two phenomena is the same: human consciousness seems predisposed to disbelieve the Good News of Jesus Christ. Christians call this an effect of original sin; their secular contemporaries call it facing the facts. Its manifestations are perennial, not surprisingly since its origins are rooted in the human psyche. Human beings left to their own devices often conclude that creation, other people, and God (or the gods) are hostile. Most of the forces outside and inside the self are presumed to be at least potentially malignant, and various expiatory remedies are sought. The 'old religions' of paganism tried to alleviate the insecurities that inevitably arise when the universe is experienced as hostile; and they seem to have had little more success than our more modern remedies of consumerism and popular psychology.

The simple fact is that it is not easy first to believe and then to go on believing the Good News proclaimed in Judaism that God really does love his creation, and the even more astonishing revelation that God has both united himself to his creation through the Incarnation, and has redeemed it—and humanity in particular—through the death and resurrection of the God–Man, Jesus Christ. Simple statement and restatement of these beliefs does not suffice: what is required is a community that manifests these beliefs in its lifestyle and visibly enters into an ever–deepening relationship with the Redeemer through lived prayer. This is what early medieval missionaries brought to pagans and lapsed Christians in the form of the Rule of St. Benedict: it may be that in our own day a rediscovery of its teaching will be as transforming for us as it was for them.

Reading the Rule of Benedict

If we wish to recover the wisdom of St. Benedict's Rule it is not enough simply to read it. As moderns we read in order to acquire information, to be 'in–formed'. In St. Benedict's day reading a sacred or spiritual text was practiced not so much for the sake of 'information,' but rather in order to be 'formed:' that is, to be inwardly changed or shaped. St. Benedict recommends in his Rule that an average of three hours per day be set aside for the practice of what he calls *lectio divina* (RB 48). These three hours were taken from the best hours of the day, times when the monk would be most alert and able to profit from the practice (8:3; 48:4-5,13-14,22). Lectio divina is a slow, meditative reading of the Scriptures or other sacred literature intended to lead the reader into intimate, personal dialogue with God. This contemplative reading is also an attentive **listening**, since reading in antiquity was almost always done aloud. Indeed, the first word of Benedict's Rule is the invitation to listen (*Obsculta, o fili - Listen, my son,* Prol.1) to the voice of God.

Thus the practice of allowing the self to be inwardly formed by the sacred text and led into the presence of God, applied equally to private reading aloud and to public reading, whether such reading took place in the monastery chapel refectory, or chapter (meeting) room. Lectio divina presupposes an alternating inner rhythm of gentle listening followed by contemplative 'rumination' and attentive presence to God, as will be described below. It is an art that was learned in childhood in Benedict's day, even by the illiterate who were expected to memorize the scriptures they heard and meditate upon them, as much as those who could read. It enabled text that was seen or heard to be taken in and made a part of the self. And, as might be expected, one of the spiritual texts read aloud publicly and regularly in Benedict's monastery was the Rule of Benedict itself (66.8).

If we are to rediscover St. Benedict's insights, we must read his Rule in a spirit of lectio divina. But to learn the art of lectio divina it is to Benedict's own sources that we must turn, especially his principal source and the one always given pride of place during the time set aside for lectio divina—namely the Bible.

Learning the Art of Lectio Divina

The earliest Christian writers who described the practice of lectio divina wrote of an oscillating rhythm of lectio—reading or 'listening to God' in the text, and *oratio*—prayer, speaking with the God who is heard.[1] Later monastic authors expanded this description to include four aspects or inner movements of lectio divina.[2] Since the terminology of these later authors has become customary in speaking of the art, we shall employ it here, modifying it where necessary.

Lectio—Reading/Listening

The art of lectio divina begins with cultivating the ability to **listen deeply**, to hear 'with the ear of our hearts' as St. Benedict writes in the Prologue to the Rule. When we read the Scriptures we should try to imitate the prophet Elijah. We should allow ourselves to become women and men who are able to listen for the still, small voice of God (I Kings 19:12); the 'faint murmuring sound' which is God's word for **us**, God's voice touching **our** hearts. This gentle listening is an 'attunement' to the presence of God in that special part of God's creation which is the Scriptures.

---

[1] St. Cyprian of Carthage (d.258) wrote in his Letter to Donatus: "Be constant as well in prayer as in reading; now speak with God, now let God speak with you, let Him instruct you in His precepts, let Him direct you." St. Ambrose of Milan wrote similarly in his *De Officiis ministrorum* (I, 20, 88) "We speak to him when we pray; we listen to him when we read the divine oracles."

[2] Principally Guigo II the Carthusian, in his *Letter on the Contemplative Life*, also known as the *Ladder of Monks*, and the Canon Hugh of St. Victor in book five of the *Didascalion*.

The cry of the prophets to ancient Israel was the joy–filled command to "Listen!"—*Sh'ma Israel: Hear, O Israel!* In lectio divina we too, heed that command and turn to the Scriptures, knowing that we must 'hear'—listen—to the voice of God, which often speaks very softly. In order to hear someone speaking softly we must learn to be silent. We must learn to love silence as St. Benedict did (Chapter 6). If we are constantly speaking or if we are surrounded with noise, we cannot hear gentle sounds. The practice of lectio divina, therefore, requires that we first quiet down in order to hear God's word to us. This is the first step of lectio divina, appropriately called *lectio*—reading.

The reading or listening which is the first step in lectio divina is very different from the speed–reading which modern Christians apply to newspapers, books and even to the Bible. Lectio is reverential listening; listening both in a spirit of silence and of awe. We are listening for the voice of God that will speak to us personally—not loudly, but intimately. In lectio we read slowly, attentively, gently listening to hear a word or phrase that is God's word for us this day.

Meditatio—Meditation

Once we have found a word or a passage in the Scriptures which speaks to us in a personal way, we must take it in and 'ruminate' on it. The image of the ruminant animal quietly chewing its cud was used in antiquity as a symbol of the Christian pondering the Word of God. Christians have always seen a scriptural invitation to lectio divina in the example of the Virgin Mary 'pondering in her heart' what she saw and heard of Christ (LUKE 2:19). For us today these images are a reminder that we must take in the word—that is, memorize it—and while gently repeating it to ourselves, allow it to interact with our thoughts, our hopes, our memories, our desires. This is the second step or stage in lectio divina—*meditatio*. Through meditatio we allow God's word to become His word for us, a word that touches us and affects us at our deepest levels.

Oratio—Prayer

The third step in lectio divina is *oratio*—prayer: prayer understood both as dialogue with God, that is, as loving conversation with the One who has invited us into His embrace; and as consecration, prayer as the priestly offering to God of parts of ourselves that we have not previously believed God wants. In this consecration–prayer we allow the word that we have taken in and on which we are pondering to touch and change our deepest selves. Just as a priest consecrates the elements of bread and wine at the Eucharist, God invites us in lectio divina to hold up our most difficult and pain–filled experiences to Him, and gently to recite over them the healing word or phrase He has given us in our lectio and meditatio. In this oratio, this consecration–prayer, we allow our real selves to be touched and changed by the word of God.

Contemplatio—Contemplation

Finally, we simply rest in the presence of the One who has used His word as a means of inviting us to accept His transforming embrace. No one who has ever been in love needs to be reminded that there are moments in loving relationships when words are unnecessary. It is the same in our relationship with God. Wordless, quiet rest in the presence of the One Who loves us has a name in the Christian tradition—*contemplatio*, contemplation. Once again we practice silence, letting go of our own words; this time simply enjoying the experience of being in the presence of God.

The Underlying Rhythm of Lectio Divina

If we are to practice lectio divina effectively, we must travel back in time to an understanding that today is in danger of being almost completely lost. In St. Benedict's day the words *action* (or *practice*, from the Greek *praktikos*) and contemplation did not describe different kinds of Christians engaging (or not engaging) in different forms of prayer and apostolates. Practice and contemplation were understood as the two poles of our underlying, ongoing spiritual rhythm: a gentle oscillation between spiritual 'activity' with regard to God and 'receptivity.'

Practice—spiritual activity—referred in ancient times to our active co-operation with God's grace in rooting out vices and allowing the virtues to flourish. The direction of spiritual activity was not outward in the sense of an apostolate, but inward: down into the depths of the soul where the Spirit of God is constantly transforming us, refashioning us in God's image. The *active* life (or *conversatio* as St. Benedict calls it in his Rule) is thus coming to see who we truly are and allowing ourselves to be remade in the way God intends.

In contemplation we cease interior spiritual *doing* and learn simply to *be*, that is to rest in the presence of our loving Father. Just as we constantly move back and forth in our exterior lives between speaking and listening, between questioning and reflecting, so in our spiritual lives we must learn to enjoy the refreshment of simply *being* in God's presence, an experience that naturally alternates (if we let it!) with our spiritual *practice*.

In ancient times contemplation was not regarded as a goal to be achieved through some method of prayer, but was simply accepted with gratitude as God's recurring gift. At intervals the Lord invites us to cease from speaking so that we can simply rest in his embrace. This is the pole of our inner spiritual rhythm called contemplation.

How different is this ancient understanding from our modern approach! Instead of recognizing that we all gently oscillate between spiritual activity and receptivity, between practice and contemplation, today we tend to set contemplation before ourselves as a goal—something we imagine we can achieve through some spiritual technique. We must be willing to sacrifice our 'goal-oriented' approach if we are to practice lectio divina, because lectio divina has no goal other than spending time with God through the medium of His word. The amount of time we spend in any aspect of lectio divina, whether it be rumination, consecration or contemplation depends on God's Spirit, not on us. Lectio divina teaches us to savor and delight in all the different flavors of God's presence, whether they be active or receptive modes of experiencing Him.

In lectio divina we offer ourselves to God; and we are people in motion. In ancient times this inner spiritual motion was described as a helix—an ascending spiral. Viewed in only two dimensions it appears as a circular motion back and forth; seen with the added dimension of time it becomes a helix, an ascending spiral by means of which we are drawn ever closer to God. The whole of our spiritual lives can be viewed in this way, as a gentle oscillation between spiritual activity and receptivity by means of which God unites us ever closer to Himself. In just the same way the steps or stages of lectio divina represent an oscillation back and forth between these spiritual poles. In lectio divina we recognize our underlying spiritual rhythm and discover many different ways of experiencing God's presence—many different ways of praying.

The Private Practice of Lectio Divina

Choose a text of the Scriptures that you wish to pray. Many Christians use in their regular lectio divina one of the daily readings from the Eucharistic liturgy; others prefer to work slowly through a particular book of the Bible. It makes no difference which text is chosen, as long as you have no set goal of 'covering' a certain amount of text: the amount of text 'covered' is in God's hands, not yours.

Place yourself in a comfortable position and allow yourself to become silent. Some Christians focus for a few moments on their breathing; other have a beloved 'prayer word' or 'prayer phrase' they gently recite in order to become inwardly silent. For some the practice known as 'centering prayer' makes a good, brief introduction to lectio divina. Use whatever method is best for you and allow yourself to enjoy silence for a few moments.

Then turn to the text and read it slowly, gently. Savor each portion of the reading, constantly listening for the 'still, small voice' of a word or phrase that says, "I am for you today." Do not expect lightning or ecstasies. In lectio divina God is teaching us to listen to Him, to seek Him in silence. He does not reach out and grab us, but softly, gently invites us ever more deeply into His presence.

Next take the word or phrase into yourself. Memorize it and slowly repeat it to yourself, allowing it to interact with your inner world of concerns, memories and ideas. Do not be afraid of 'distractions.' Memories or thoughts are simply parts of yourself which, when they rise up during lectio divina, are asking to be given to God with the rest of your inner self. Allow this inner pondering, this rumination, to invite you into dialogue with God.

Then, speak to God. Whether you use words or ideas or images or all three, is not important. Interact with God as you would with one who you know loves and accepts you. And give to Him what you have discovered in yourself during your experience of meditatio. Experience yourself as the priest that you are. Experience God using the word or phrase that He has given you as a means of blessing, of transforming the ideas and memories, which your pondering on His word has awakened. Give to God what you have found within your heart.

Finally, simply rest in God's embrace. And when He invites you to return to your pondering of His word or to your inner dialogue with Him, do so. Learn to use words when words are helpful, and to let go of words when they are no longer necessary. Rejoice in the knowledge that God is with you in both words and silence, in spiritual activity and inner receptivity.

Sometimes in lectio divina you will return several times to the printed text, either to savor the literary context of the word or phrase that God has given, or to seek a new word or phrase to ponder. At other times only a single word or phrase will fill the whole time set aside for lectio divina. It is not necessary to anxiously assess the quality of your lectio divina as if you were 'performing'. Lectio divina has no goal other than that of being in the presence of God by praying the Scriptures.

This, then, is a modern adaptation of the attentive, contemplative approach to reading and hearing sacred texts that underlies St. Benedict's Rule. It is clear that he expected his Rule to be memorized and pondered in the same way that the scriptures are pondered: Chapter 4, 'The Instruments of Good Works,' and Chapter 72, 'On Good Zeal' have a delightful, sing-song cadence when read aloud in Latin, making them easy to memorize and then to recite or chant to oneself while at work or at leisure. In this translation we have included the traditional divisions of the Rule into brief, consecutive sections for daily reading that allow the Rule to be read through three times each year, a practice Benedict particularly recommended to new members of the community (58.9-16). Spending a little time each day on a different portion of the Rule can allow its richness to be slowly acquired and savored. In the Select Bibliography at the end of this Introduction are listed several books that can be of assistance both in learning the art of *lectio divina* and in practicing it daily, using the Rule of Benedict.

Christian Life According to the
Rule of Benedict

The Rule of Benedict presents a specific way for Christians to live in response to the Gospel. Christians who bind themselves by vows according to the teaching of the Rule are called monks or nuns if they live in monasteries, and oblates or confraters if they are laypeople living in the world. Their life is characterized by a rhythm of consecration—a movement back and forth between prayer and work that enables them to experience the whole of life as charged with God's glory, and to offer that life back to God in prayer.

The basis for life according to the Rule is the offering of one's self to God in a particular praying community. This is very important. There is no such thing as 'generic' monasticism: each monastery has its own unique characteristics and its own adaptation of Benedict's Rule; each will have its own rhythm and form of work and prayer, and its own relationship with the local Church. One makes vows, whether as a monk, nun, oblate or confrater, not to a concept or an ideal, but to the specific way of life of a particular monastery. The Latin word *conversatio* means 'way of life'; and Benedictines vow *conversatio morum,* (58.17) commitment to the unique way of life of a particular monastery.

In promising to remain faithful to their monastic commitment for life, Benedictine nuns and monks also promise not to flee their particular monastery for 'greener pastures:' this is called the vow of stability (58.15-17). It is not easy to remain in committed, intimate relationship with other people for life. Pretense and defense mechanisms inevitably crumble, and one is left with the painful awareness that one is seen and known for what one is, just as clearly and vulnerably as one sees and knows the others. But Benedict promised that Christ is present in guests, (53.1) in the abbot, (2.2; 63.13) in the sick and those who tend them (36.14), in short, in each person. Benedictines vow to endure the inner trauma of ongoing interpersonal relationships with God's help, and in persevering through them to discover Christ present in each of their brothers and sisters.

As difficult as the concept of stability is for modern Christians, the Benedictine vow of obedience (Chapters 6 & 68) is even harder. From the very first paragraph of his Rule, St. Benedict makes it clear that this way of life is for those "who are ready to renounce self-will" (Prol.3). Nothing is more central to popular contemporary understandings of the self than the notions of independence and fulfillment of individual potential. Part of our modern difficulty in committed relationships is the limitations they impose on the partners. The partner in any intimate relationship is eventually experienced as a limitation to personal freedom, perhaps even as an obstacle to inner growth. And this may be true. But in the community envisaged by Benedict, all go "together to eternal life" (72.12); and rather than seeking what is best for himself, each must learn to seek "what is best for the other" (72.7). Individual differences should be taken into account; (2.22-24) but the ultimate goal is the same for each, namely "what eye has not seen, nor ear heard" (4.77; I Cor.2:9). Thus the real fulfillment of individual potential lies beyond this life, and may well include hardships and frequent limitation of freedom: "may we by patience participate in the passion of Christ; that we may deserve also to be partakers of his kingdom" (Prol. 50).

More concretely, Benedictines live under the authority of an abbot or abbess who is believed to "hold the place of Christ." Although in recent centuries monastic superiors have been elected by their communities, this was not always the case. And even today the monastery is not in any meaningful sense a democracy or a republic. The Rule of St. Benedict provides a model for the arrangement of the physical and cultural affairs of the monastery and the role of the abbot as its temporal and spiritual father. It is clear from the Rule that, ideally, temporal matters are informed by and integrated with the spiritual, and much of the work of the abbot is in pursuit of this ideal.

Benedict and the Master

All that is known of St. Benedict's life is found in Book II of the *Dialogues* of Pope St. Gregory the Great, a work written around the year 600, more than half a century after Benedict's death. None of the literature or the famous people of Benedict's own generation mention him. We are thus dependent solely on a document that is not at all 'biography' in the modern sense: the expressed purpose of the *Dialogues* was to strengthen the religious fervor of its readers by presenting them with examples of holiness found in local, contemporary saints. Although Gregory maintains that his evidence was obtained from eye-witnesses, his stated purpose is to edify the faithful, not to satisfy the curious. Thus there are almost no precise dates that can be assigned to events in Benedict's life.

Born about the year 480, in Nursia, Italy, the young Benedict was sent to school in Rome. In addition to the moral depravity which Gregory claims disgusted Benedict, the young man must have witnessed something of the collapse of traditional social and political structures which was taking place in the Christian West. In Rome he underwent a religious conversion that convinced him to become a hermit.

After several years, first in partial then in complete solitude in Subiaco, he was made superior of a monastic community which soon attempted to assassinate him for his strictness. He returned to Subiaco and founded twelve small monasteries of twelve monks each. He later left Subiaco and founded the Abbey of Monte Cassino, about eighty miles south of Rome, where he remained until his death around the year 540. It was probably as abbot of Monte Cassino that Benedict wrote his Rule, which is the only document from his pen we possess. The principal source Benedict used in writing his Rule has only recently been identified; and in order to understand the relationship between these two Rules, we must move ahead to when the Western empire began to show signs of reviving.

In the early ninth century, nearly four hundred years after the death of Benedict of Nursia, St. Benedict of Aniane, a monk who had served in the court of Pepin, was asked by the Emperor Charlemagne to assist in the reform of Frankish monasticism. He assembled and published a collection of all known monastic rules, intending to demonstrate the superiority of the Rule of Benedict and thus encourage its widespread acceptance and use. His *Concordia Regularurn* included a document of unknown date and authorship entitled *The Rule of the Master*. It is three times longer than the Rule of Benedict, but it is clear on even a cursory reading that the two documents are closely related. Large portions of the two Rules are almost identical; and although the anonymous Master's style is tedious and given to detailed legislation on what often seem to be insignificant matters, it is impossible to compare the two documents and not be convinced that one of the authors must have used the other's work as his model.

For centuries it was assumed that Benedict's Rule had been written first, and that the Rule of the Master was a sort of second–rate extended commentary on it. But in this century detailed textual and linguistic studies of the two Rules have convinced most scholars that the relationship is the other way around: Benedict used the Rule of the Master as the template for his own rule. For those who wished to view Benedict as a creative genius in the modern sense, this revelation has come as a crushing blow. Benedictines have always delighted in the rich tapestry of interwoven patristic and scriptural texts that characterize the Rule: Benedict's presumed familiarity with the sources he quotes has served as an inspiration for monks throughout the centuries. The discovery that Benedict did not create, but rather transplanted and adapted this richness, has forced those who love his Rule to rethink what they mean by Benedict's 'genius'. [3]

The uniqueness and greatness of Benedict's contribution does not lie in his originality: indeed, for a monk of Benedict's day the statement that he had contributed something 'completely original' would have sounded more like an accusation than a compliment. Monastic wisdom did not consist in making original contributions, but rather in listening attentively and reverently to the Word of God in Scripture and Tradition, and then prayerfully, meditatively, in what we have here called a spirit of lectio divina, offering to

---

[3] A few Benedictine scholars have avoided this dilemma by suggesting that Benedict wrote the *Rule of the Master* in his youth and then, after mature reflection, revised it as the Rule which bears his name. This hypothesis not only raises textual difficulties with regard to the different ways 'Benedict' used patristic sources in the two rules; but also it posits an incredible transformation in Benedict's outlook and temperament.

the next generation those portions of the tradition that speak the truths of the Gospel most clearly. This is precisely what Benedict did. He took a document obsessed with minutiae and carefully, lovingly pruned it to one-third its original length. He obviously omitted large portions of the text; but in the retained sections his reverence for his ponderous template is apparent: he edits by judiciously deleting a word or a phrase here, by adding a word or a sentence there, leaving the original intact wherever he can. Part of Benedict's genius lies in his respectful adaptation of a text that later monks would deride: he took what later generations would call dross and made it shine like gold.

An example or two will give some indication of Benedict's intentions and method. In Chapter 6, 'On Humility,' the Master presents the traditional monastic image of a spiritual 'ladder' with its first rung at the Fear of the Lord, leading upwards through such steps as renunciation of self-will, obedience, patient endurance, and taciturnity, to attainment of the love of the Lord. The Master created this ladder from the 'signs of humility' that Cassian had described[4] nearly a hundred years previously. Benedict in his turn modifies the Master's ladder, subtly but significantly. For the Master, love of the Lord is achieved only after much endurance and spiritual renunciation. Benedict, however, recognizes that love must be both the goal and the motive: for acts of heroic virtue are worth nothing unless they are motivated by love and inspired by God's grace. Thus he leaves the order of the rungs the same as in the *Rule of the Master*, but he inserts the phrase 'for the love of God' at the third of the twelve

---

[4] Cassian, *Institutes* 4.39–43.

steps. In Benedict's version of the Ladder of Humility love is already present at the lower steps and reaches its full fruition with the casting out of fear (6.67).

One of the principal goals of this edition of the Rule is to enable readers to appreciate how Benedict reshaped the Rule of the Master and so to acquire a sense of the extent and nature of Bendict's own contributions. In this edition of the Rule bold-face type indicates text that is unique to Benedict; normal type indicates that the text is common to both the Rule of the Master and Benedict's Rule. In the first seven chapters of his Rule, Benedict borrows heavily from the Rule of the Master; thus in these chapters bold-face type appears less frequently, and when present it indicates how Benedict has modified the Master's text. In chapter eight and onwards, bold-face type predominates, indicating that, although Benedict is probably still using the Master's text as a working document, he is either expressing his own ideas or introducing material from other monastic or patristic texts. The reader may wish to consult the *RB 80* edition of Benedict's Rule (published by Liturgical Press, Collegeville, Minnesota) to see exactly which other ancient sources Benedict is using in any given chapter.

At the beginning of most sections of the Latin text in this edition is a reference to the parallel chapter(s) in the Rule of the Master. This is to enable the reader to compare the Rule of Benedict with the corresponding chapter in the Rule of the Master, which is available in English translation from Cistercian Publications, (see the Select Bibliography on page xxvii). Further notes on the typographical conventions used in this edition are given after the Bibliography.

The Rule Through the Centuries

Cardinal Basil Hume, a modern Benedictine monk and Archbishop of Westminster, once observed that the only prophecy St. Benedict ever made about his monastery of Monte Cassino was that it would one day be destroyed.[5] That prophecy, namely that the buildings would be destroyed but that the monks would escape,[6] is perhaps a fitting symbol for the relationship between the Rule of Benedict and the monks, nuns, and laypeople who derive inspiration and direction from that Rule.

Benedictine monks and nuns tend to delight in ancient abbeys and distinguished community pedigrees: but the truth is that Benedictine communities are constantly being created and are constantly disappearing. Few monasteries in history have endured in full vigor for more than two or three centuries. Eventually the communities grow affluent and influential, monastic observance becomes lax, and the orginal foundations either become extinct or are reformed, sometimes so thoroughly that the reform amounts to a new foundation. It is not abbeys and monastic congregations that provide the real continuity seen in the history of Benedictines: rather it is the vigor and power of the Rule itself.

According to tradition, the monks of Monte Cassino escaped to Rome with the autograph copy of Benedict's Rule.[7] Nothing certain is known of their

---

[5] Homily for the Sesquemillenial celebration of the Feast of St. Benedict, given at Westminster Cathedral, 1980.

[6] *Dialogues* Book II.17.

[7] This tradition is reported by Paul the Deacon (c.720–c.800) *History of the Langobard People* 4,17: the sources he used in compiling this history are no longer extant.

fate; however the precious manuscript they brought
with them may well have been returned to Monte
Cassino when it was restored two hundred years later.
Throughout this time, copies of the Rule were probably
made and variously distributed; but there would be
nothing that could properly be called a Benedictine
'Order' for several centuries. Monasticism had existed
in the West for nearly two hundred years before
Benedict; and the most common practice in
monasteries from the sixth through the eighth centuries
was to use several monastic rules, the so–called *regula
mixta,* to regulate monastic observance. Legends
abound of early 'Benedictines' such as St. Gregory
the Great (c.540–604) and St. Augustine of Canterbury
(died c.605) who were supposed to have introduced
Benedict's Rule to different communities; but there is
no certain evidence for its widespread popularity prior
to the seventh century, nearly two centuries after
Benedict's death.

Celtic missionary–monks in the seventh century
used Benedict's Rule side–by–side with the much
stricter Rules of St. Columban. In their monasteries
on the Continent the Rule of Benedict slowly proved
itself, possibly due to its more balanced, compassionate
approach; and it gradually displaced other rules. In
England, Benedict's Rule was one of the 'Roman
usages' for which there was a growing zeal throughout
the seventh century; and there too it replaced older
Celtic usages. In the early ninth century St. Benedict
of Aniane, mentioned above, championed its use under
the patronage of Charlemagne and his son Louis.
Although Benedict of Aniane's reform did not survive
the fall of Charlemagne's empire, his emphasis on the
Rule of Benedict as the sole rule for monks became

one of the guiding principles of the great Cluniac reform of the tenth century: and from this period onward one can safely speak of 'Benedictines' who regarded the Rule of Benedict as their principal guide for living out the commands of the Gospel.

In a sense, however, the tradition of a *regula mixta* still prevails today. It has been said, perhaps accurately, that there has been no monastery since Benedict's own that has used only his rule as its guide. Alongside the Rule, certainly from the time of Benedict of Aniane and probably before, monasteries have written up their own modifications and amplifications of the Rule in customaries or constitutions. These documents represent the necessity of continuing, in light of Benedict's example, the work he began in modifying the Rule of the Master. In every generation the literal precepts of the Rule must serve as the basis for a communal lectio divina that results in highlighting certain aspects, and often de–emphasizing other elements according to the Spirit working in the Church in any given age. But even though monks of every century have had their own unique and sometimes amusing interpretations of it, the Rule itself has remained, and for good reason.

There have been several points in history when Benedictine monasticism as an institution seemed in danger of extinction. Invasions by Norsemen and Saracens in the ninth century, the plagues of the fourteenth and fifteenth centuries, the Reformation of the sixteenth, and the Napoleonic suppressions of the nineteenth centuries, all came close to or actually succeeded in extinguishing Benedictine monasticism in parts of Europe. But almost invariably, when it became possible for communities to be refounded according to the Rule of Benedict, they were. Sometimes this was done by communities that had survived the devastations; but even in the absence of a living monastic tradition, the Rule by itself has sometimes provided the basis for a monastic rebirth. One of the most influential modern Benedictine congregations, that of Solesmes, was founded by a diocesan priest who served no monastic apprenticeship and made no novitiate. He studied the Rule, meditated on its precepts, investigated its history, gathered about him a group of like–minded men and founded a community that was eventually accorded legitimate status by the Church.

In other words, study of the Rule of Benedict has, in the present as well as in the past, provided the basis for the structure and life of many and various Christian communities. Thus the Rule is instrumental in bringing to the lives of human beings a very tangible appreciation of our redemption in Jesus Christ.

✝

SELECT BIBLIOGRAPHY

1. Scholarly Reference

La Règle de Saint Benoît, in six volumes ed. Jean Neufville, notes and tr. by Adalbert de Vogüé, Sources Chrétiennes 181-186, (Paris, Les Éditions du Cerf, 1971-72). Critical edition of the Latin text with textual apparatus, includes meticulous indication of the relationship between the Rules of Benedict and the Master for chapters 1-7; also includes facing French translation and unsurpassed commentary and notes by Fr. de Vogüé.

RB 1980, The Rule of St. Benedict in Latin and English, ed. Timothy Fry, *et al.,* Liturgical Press (Collegeville, 1980). Based principally on the critical edition described above, this is the most comprehensive and indispensable resource on the Rule of Benedict available in English. In addition to scholarly discussions of the Rule, the introductory chapters and appendices provide a valuable introduction to monastic history and spirituality.

La Règle du Maître, in three volumes; ed., tr., and notes by Adalbert de Vogüé, Sources Chrétiennes 105-107, (Paris, Les Éditions du Cerf, 1964-65). Critical edition with textual apparatus, facing French tr. and detailed notes.

The Rule of The Master, tr. Luke Eberle, intro. Adalbert de Vogüé, Cistercian Publications, (Kalamazoo, 1977). This is the only English translation of the Rule of the Master available at present. While it includes biblical and some patristic citations, the notes are generally too brief and too few for this work to be useful on its own: it should be read either with the notes from the critical edition above, or (where possible) with notes from the parallel passages in the *RB 1980.*

2. Early Monastic Texts

The Institutes and Conferences of John Cassian: no complete
English translation exists at present: the most complete is
in vol. 11 of *The Nicene and Post-Nicene Fathers, second
series,* (available on the Internet). Selected conferences
are also available in *Western Asceticism,* ed. Owen
Chadwick, Westminster Press (Louisville, 1988); *John
Cassian, Conferences,* tr. Colm Luibheid, Paulist Press
(Mahwah,1985, *The Classics of Western Spirituality*).

The Rule of Basil, Catholic University of America Press
(Washington DC, 1950, *The Fathers of the Church);* this
includes only Basil's *Longer Rule.*

The Rule of the Four Fathers and the Regula Orientalis, tr.
Franklin *et al.,* Liturgical Press (Collegeville, 1981, *Early
Monastic Rules*).

The Life of Antony: editions include: vol. 4 of *The Nicene and
Post-Nicene Fathers, second series,* (available on the
Internet); *The Life of Antony and the Letter to Marcellinus,*
tr. R.C. Gregg, Paulist Press (Mahwah, 1980, *Classics of
Western Spirituality*); *The Life of St. Antony,* tr. R.T.
Meyer, Newman (Washington DC, 1950, *Ancient
Christian Writers 10).*

The Lives and *Sayings of the Desert Fathers,* are available in
the following editions: *Western Asceticism,* ed. Owen
Chadwick, Westminster Press (Louisville, 1988); *The
Sayings of the Desert Fathers,* tr. Benedicta Ward,
Cistercian Publications (Kalamazoo, 1975, *Cistercian
Studies 59);The Lives of the Desert Fathers* tr. N. Russell,
Cistercian Pub., (1980, *Cistercian Studies 34*); The
Lausiac History, Palladius, tr. R.T. Meyer, Paulist Press
(Mahwah, 1964, *Ancient Christian Writers No. 34*).

Gregory the Great–The Life of Saint Benedict, commentary by Adalbert de Vogüé, St. Bede's Publications, (Petersham,1993).

3. Benedictine Spirituality

The Rule of St. Benedict, A Commentary, P. DeLatte, Burns & Oates (London, 1921).

Benedictine Monachism, Cuthbert Butler, Longmans, Green & Co. (London, 2nd edn. 1924).

The Way to God According to the Rule of St. Benedict, Emmanuel Heufelder, Cistercian Pub. (Kalamazoo, 1983, Cistercian Studies 49), this is a translation of *Der Weg zu Gott*.

Reading Saint Benedict, Reflections on the Rule, Adalbert de Vogüé, Cistercian Pub. (1991, *Cistercian Studies 151*).

The Rule of Saint Benedict, a Doctrinal and Spiritual Commentary, Adalbert de Vogüé, Cistercian Pub. (1983, *Cistercian Studies 54*), translation of *La Règle de Saint Benoît VII, Commentaire doctrinal et spirituel*.

Community and Abbot in the Rule of Saint Benedict, Adalbert de Vogüé, two volumes, Cistercian Pub., (1979, 1988, *Cistercian Studies 5/1* and *5/2*), a translation of *La Communauté et l'Abbé dans la Règle de saint Benoît*.

Preferring Christ, A Devotional Workbook and Commentary on the Rule of St. Benedict, Norvene Vest, Source Books (Trabuco Canyon, 1991), directed especially at laity and oblates of monastic communities.

ABOUT THIS EDITION

As has already been described, one purpose of this edition of the Rule is to make available to the general public a text which facilitates comparison between the Rule of Benedict and the Rule of the Master. In this edition bold–face type indicates text that is unique to Benedict; normal type indicates text that is common to both the Rule of the Master and Benedict's Rule.

This project was inspired by the critical edition of the Rule of St. Benedict edited by Frs. Adalbert De Vogüé, o.s.b, and Jean Neufville, o.s.b, published in seven volumes by Sources Chrétiennes in Paris. This work, to which all serious students of Benedict's Rule should refer, describes in detail the relationship between the respective rules of Benedict and the Master. To this end the editors provide both an extensive commentary and, for chapters 1–7, a text-format that depicts Benedict's dependence on the Master in meticulous detail.

The purpose of this present edition, however, is much more modest and our typographical conventions are therefore quite different from those employed by Frs. De Vogüé and Neufville. Our purpose here is not so much to emphasize Benedict's dependence on the Master, a point that is now almost universally accepted, but rather to provide a resource that emphasizes Benedict's unique contribution. **Thus we have highlighted, both in Latin and in English, the text which Benedict does *not* quote from the Master's rule,** and which therefore reflects either his own ideas or his independent use of other monastic and patristic sources.

If the reader wishes to delve further into the question of how Benedict uses sources other than the Scriptures, it will be necessary to consult either the critical edition of Frs. De Vogüé and Neufville, or the magisterial *RB 80* edition of the Rule, published by Liturgical Press. The latter is both easier to obtain and less costly than the critical edition, on which it is very closely based. The *RB 80* includes a commentary, footnotes indicating Benedict's (and the Master's) use of patristic sources, and valuable introductions and appendices.

In conclusion, a few points should be made concerning the English translation of this present edition. My principal goal has been to facilitate easy reference back and forth between the English and Latin text for those whose background in Latin may be limited, and thereby to encourage greater familiarity with Benedict's Latin text. To this end I have tried to use English words related to or based on the Latin terms used by Benedict, and I have tried wherever possible to preserve his word-order and sentence structure. This has resulted in an English text that occasionally employs archaic vocabulary and syntax. It is my sincere hope that the effect of this will be to encourage the reader to rely less on this (or any vernacular) translation, and to savor instead in its original tongue the rich treasures of the Rule of St. Benedict.

LUKE DYSINGER, O.S.B.
VALYERMO, 1996

REGULA SANCTI BENEDICTI

THE RULE OF SAINT BENEDICT

(RM Pr.1-11, 19-22; ThP6,24-53, 69-79; ThS1-4)

PROLOGUS

[1] *Obsculta, o fili,* praecepta magistri, *et inclina aurem* cordis tui et *admonitionem* pii *patris libenter* excipe et efficaciter comple; [2] ut ad eum per obedientiae laborem redeas, a quo per inobedientiae desidiam recesseras.

[3] Ad te ergo, nunc mihi sermo dirigitur, quisquis abrenuntians propriis voluntatibus, Domino Christo vero Regi militaturus, oboedientiae fortissima atque praeclara arma sumis.

[4] In primis, ut quidquid agendum inchoas bonum, ab eo perfici instantissima oratione deposcas; [5] ut, qui nos iam in filiorum dignatus est numero computare, non debet aliquando de malis actibus nostris contristari.

[6] Ita enim ei omni tempore de bonis suis in nobis parendum est, ut non solum iratus pater suos non aliquando filios exheredet, [7]sed nec ut metuendus dominus, irritatus a malis nostris, ut nequissimos servos perpetuam tradat ad poenam qui eum sequi noluerint ad gloriam.

(RM ThS 5-9)

[8] Exsurgamus ergo tandem aliquando, excitante nos scriptura ac dicente: *Hora est iam nos de somno surgere,* [9] et apertis oculis nostris ad deificum lumen, attonitis auribus audiamus divina cotidie clamans quid nos admonet vox, dicens: [10] *Hodie si vocem eius audieritis, nolite obdurare corda vestra.* [11] Et iterum: *Qui habet aures audiendi audiat quid spiritus dicat ecclesiis.*

Jan 1; May 2; Sept 1

THE PROLOGUE

[1] *Listen, O my son* to the precepts of the master, *and incline the ear* of your heart: *willingly* receive and faithfully fulfill the *admonition* of your *loving father;* (CF. PROV. 1:8, 4:20, 6:20) [2] that you may return by the labor of obedience to him from whom you had departed through the laziness of disobedience.

[3] To you therefore, my words are now addressed, whoever you are, that through renouncing your own will you may fight for the Lord Christ, the true king, by taking up the strong and bright weapons of obedience.

[4] First, whenever you begin any good work, beg of him with most earnest prayer to perfect it; [5] so that he who has now granted us the dignity of being counted among the number of his sons may not at any time be grieved by our evil deeds.

[6] For we must always so serve him with the good things he has given us, that not only may he never, as an angry father, disinherit his children; [7] but may never as a dread Lord, incensed by our sins, deliver us to everlasting punishment as most wicked servants who would not follow him to glory.

Jan 2; May 3; Sept 2

[8] Let us then at last arise, since the Scripture arouses us saying: *It is now time for us to rise from sleep* (ROM. 13:11). [9] And let us open our eyes to the deifying light; let us attune our ears to what the divine voice admonishes us, daily crying out: [10] *Today if you hear his voice, harden not your hearts* (Ps. 95:7-8). [11] And again, *You who have ears to hear, hear what the Spirit says to the churches* (REV. 2:7).

3

[12] **Et** quid **dicit?** *Venite, filii, audite me; timorem Domini docebo vos.* [13] *Currite dum lumen vitae habetis, ne tenebrae mortis vos comprehendant.*

(RM ThS 10-16)

[14] Et quaerans Dominus in multitudine populi qui haec clamat operarium suum, iterum dicit: [15] *Quis est homo qui vult vitam, et cupit videre dies bonos?*

[16] Quod si tu audiens respondeas: Ego; dicit tibi Deus: [17] Si vis habere veram et perpetuam vitam, *prohibe linguam tuam a malo, et labia tua ne loquantur dolum. Deverte a malo et fac bonum, inquire pacem et sequere eam.*

[18] Et cum haec feceritis, *oculi* mei *super* vos *et aures* meas **ad** *preces* vestras, *et antquam me invocetis dicam* vobis: *Ecce adsum.*

[19] Quid dulcius nobis ab hac voce Domini invitantis nos, fratres **carissimi**? [20] Ecce pietate sua demonstrat nobis Dominus viam vitae.

(RM ThS 17-27)

[21] *Succinctis* ergo *fide* vel observantia bonorum actuum *lumbis* nostris, per ducatum *evangelii* pergamus itinera eius, ut mereamur eum *qui* nos *vocavit in regnum suum* videre.

[22] In cuius regni tabernaculo si volumus habitare, nisi illuc bonis actibus curritur, minime pervenitur.

12 **And** what **does he say?** *Come my sons, listen to me, I will teach you the fear of the Lord* (PSALM 34:12).
13 *Run while you have the light of life, lest the darkness of death seize hold of you* (JOHN 12:35).

Jan 3;   May 4;   Sept 3

14 And the Lord, seeking his own workman in the multitude of the people to whom he cries out, says again: 15 *Who is it who desires life, and longs to see good days?* (PSALM 34:12)

16And if you, hearing him, respond, "I am the one!" God says to you: 17 "If you desire true and everlasting life, *keep your tongue from evil and your lips from speaking deceit. Turn aside from evil and do good; seek peace and pursue it* (PSALM 34:13-14).

18 And when you have done these things, my *eyes will be upon* you, *and* my *ears towards your prayers; and before you call upon me, I will say to you, 'Behold, I am here'* (ISAIAH 58:9).

19 What can be sweeter to us than this voice of the Lord inviting us, **dearest** brothers? 20 Behold in his loving kindness the Lord shows us the way of life.

Jan 4;   May 5;   Sept 4

21 *Having* therefore *girded* our *loins with faith* and the performance of good works, with *the Gospel* as guide (EPHESIANS 6:14-15) let us walk in his paths, that we may deserve to see him *who has called us into his kingdom* (I THESSALONIANS 2:12).

22 Is the tent of this kingdom where we wish to dwell? Unless by our good deeds we run there, we shall never arrive there.

²³ Sed interrogemus cum propheta Dominum dicentes ei: *Domine, quis habitabit in tabernaculo tuo, aut quis requiescet in monte sancto tuo?*

²⁴ Post hanc interrogationem, fratres, audiamus Dominum respondentem et ostendentem nobis viam ipsius tabernaculi, ²⁵ dicens: *Qui ingreditur sine macula et operatur iustitiam;* ²⁶ *qui loquitur veritatem in corde suo,* ²⁷ *qui non egit dolum in lingua sua; qui non fecit proximo suo malum, qui opprobrium non accepit adversus proximum suum;*

²⁸ qui *malignum* diabolum aliqua suadentem sibi, cum ipsa suasione sua a *conspectibus* cordis sui respuens, *deduxit ad nihilum,* et *parvulos* cogitatos eius *tenuit et allisit ad* Christum;

²⁹ qui *timentes Dominum,* de bona observantia sua non se reddunt elatos, sed ipsa in se bona non a se posse sed a Domino fieri existamantes, ³⁰ operantem in se Dominum *magnificant,* illud cum propheta dicentes: *Non nobis, Domine, non nobis, sed nomini tuo da gloriam;*

³¹ **sicut** nec Paulus apostolus de praedicatione sua sibi aliquid imputavit, dicens: *Gratia Dei sum id quod sum;* ³² et **iterum** ipse **dicit:** *Qui gloriatur, in Domino glorietur.*

(RM ThS 39-44)

³³ Unde et Dominus in Evangelio ait: *Qui audit verba mea haec et facit ea, similabo eum viro sapienti qui aedificavit domum suam super petram;* ³⁴ *venerunt flumina, flaverunt venti, et impegerunt in domum illam, et non cecidit,* **quia** *fundata erat super petram.*

[23] But let us with the Prophet inquire of the Lord, saying to him: *Lord, who shall dwell in your tent, or who shall rest upon your holy mountain?* (PSALM 15:1)

[24] After this question, brothers, let us hear the Lord responding, showing us the way to his tent, [25] saying: *One who walks without stain and works justice;* [26] *one who speaks truth in his heart,* [27] *who has not practiced deceit with his tongue; one who has done no evil to his neighbor, and has not believed false accusations against his neighbor* (PSALM 15:2-3);

[28] one who has expelled the *malignant* devil together with all his advice and persuasiveness out of *the sight* of his heart, *casting him to naught;* and has *grasped* his *infantile* thoughts *and hurled them against* Christ (PSALM 14:4; 136:9).

[29] These are they who, *fearing the Lord*, are not elated over their own good observance; rather, knowing that the good which is in them comes not from themselves but from the Lord, [30] they *magnify* (PSALM 15:4) the Lord who works in them, saying with the Prophet: *Not unto us, O Lord, not to us, but to your name give the glory.* (PSALM 115:1)

[31] **In this way** the Apostle Paul imputed nothing of his preaching to himself, but said: *By the grace of God I am what I am.* (I CORINTHIANS 15:10) [32] And **again** he **says:** *He who glories, let him glory in the Lord.* (II CORINTHIANS 10:17)

Jan 5;   May 6;   Sept 5

[33] Hence also the Lord says in the Gospel: *He who hears these words of mine and does them is like a wise man who built his house upon rock:* [34] *the floods came, the winds blew and beat upon that house, and it did not fall; because it was founded upon rock.* (MATTHEW 7:24-5)

^{35} Haec complens Dominus expectat nos cotidie his suis sanctis monitis factis nos respondere debere. ^{36} Ideo nobis propter emendationem malorum huius vitae dies ad indutias relaxantur, ^{37} dicente apostolo: *An nescis quia patientia Dei ad paenitentiam te adducit?* ^{38} Nam pius Dominus dicit: *Nolo mortem peccatoris, sed convertatur et vivat.*

(RM ThS 29-38)

^{39} Cum ergo interrogassemus Dominum, fratres, de habitatore tabernaculi eius, audivimus habitandi praeceptum, sed si compleamus habitatoris officium.

^{40} Ergo praeparanda sunt corda nostra et corpora sanctae praeceptorum oboedientiae militanda, ^{41} et quod minus habet in nos natura possibile, rogemus Dominum ut gratiae suae iubeat nobis adiutorium ministrare.

^{42} Et si, fugientes gehennae poenas, ad vitam volumus pervenire perpetuam, ^{43} dum adhuc vacat et in hoc corpore sumus et haec omnia per hanc lucis vitam vacat implere ^{44} currendum et agendum est modo quod in perpetuo nobis expediat.

(RM ThS 45-46)

^{45} Constituenda est ergo nobis dominici schola servitii. ^{46} In qua institutione nihil asperum nihil grave nos constituturos speramus; ^{47} sed et si quid paululum restrictius, dictante aequitatis ratione, propter emendationem vitiorum vel conservationem caritatis processerit, ^{48} non ilico pavore perterritus refugias viam salutis quae non est nisi angusto initio incipienda.

[35] With these admonitions concluded, the Lord **is waiting** daily for us to respond by our deeds to his holy guidance. [36] Therefore, in order that we may amend our evil ways, the days of our lives have been lengthened as a reprieve, [37] as the Apostle says: *Do you not know that the patience of God is leading you to repentance?* (ROMANS 2:4) [38] For the loving Lord says: *I do not desire the death of a sinner, but that he should be converted and live.* (EZEKIEL 33:11)

Jan 6;   May 7;   Sept 6

[39] Therefore, brethren, having asked the Lord who is to dwell in his tent, we have heard his commands to those who are to dwell there: it thus remains for us to complete the duties of those who dwell there.

[40] Therefore our hearts and bodies must be prepared to fight in holy obedience to his commands. [41] And for that which is hardly possible to us by nature, let us ask God to supply by the help of his grace.

[42] And if we wish to reach eternal life, escaping the pains of hell, then [43]—while there is yet time, while we are still in the flesh and are able to fulfill all these things by this light of life given to us— [44] we must run and perform now what will profit us for all eternity.

Jan 7;   May 8;   Sept 7

[45] We have therefore, to establish a school of the Lord's service. [46] **In instituting it we hope to establish nothing harsh or oppressive.** [47] **But if anything is somewhat strictly laid down, according to the dictates of equity and for the amendment of vices or for the preservation of love;** [48] **do not therefore flee in dismay from the way of salvation, which cannot be other than narrow at the beginning.** (*cf.* MATTHEW 7:14)

9

[49] **Processu vero conversationis et fidei**, *dilatato corde* inenarrabili dilectionis dulcedine *curritur via mandatorum* Dei, [50] ut ab ipsius numquam magisterio discedentes, *in* **eius** *doctrinam usque ad mortem* in monasterio *perseverantes, passionibus Christi* per patientiam *participemur, ut et* regno *eius* mereamur *esse* **consortes.** Amen.

[INCIPIT TEXTUS REGULAE]
[Regula appellatur ab hoc quod oboedientum dirigat mores]

(RM 1:1-5)

I   DE GENERBUS MONACHORUM

[1] Monachorum quattuor esse genera manifestum est. [2] Primum coenobitarum, hoc est monasteriale, militans sub regula vel abbate.

[3] Deinde secundum genus est anachoritarum, id est eremitarum, horum qui non conversationis fervore novicio, sed monasterii probatione diuturna, [4] qui didicerunt contra diabolum multorum solacio iam docti pugnare, [5] et bene exstructi fraterna ex acie ad singularem pugnam eremi, securi iam sine consolatione alterius, sola manu vel brachio contra vitia carnis vel cogitationum, Deo **auxiliante**, pugnare sufficiunt.

⁴⁹ Truly as we advance in this way of life and faith, *our hearts open wide,* and we *run* with unspeakable sweetness of love *on the path of* God's commandments (PSALM 119:32), ⁵⁰ so that, never departing from his guidance, but *persevering in* his *teaching* (ACTS 2:42) in the monastery *until death,* (PHILIPPIANS 2:8) we may by patience *participate in the passion of Christ; that* we may deserve also to be **partakers** of *his* kingdom. Amen. (*cf.* I PETER 4:13; ROMANS 8:17)

[HERE BEGINS THE TEXT OF THE RULE]
[It is called a rule because it directs the lives of those who obey it.]

Jan 8; May 9; Sept 8

CHAPTER I: THE VARIOUS KINDS of MONKS

¹ It is clear that there are four kinds of monks. ² First are the cenobites: that is, those who live in monasteries and serve under a rule and an abbot.

³ The second kind are the anchorites, that is hermits: no longer in the first fervor of their way of life, they have undergone long testing in the monastery; ⁴ they have been trained to fight against the devil through the help and training of many others. ⁵ And well-armed, they go forth from the battle line held by their brethren to the solitary combat of the desert; now able to fight safely without the support of another, single-handed against the vices of flesh and thoughts with God's **help**.

11

(RM 1:6-9, 13-14, 68, 74-75)

[6] Tertium vero monachorum **tae**terrimum genus est sarabaitarum, qui nulla regula approbati, experientia magistra, *sicut aurum fornacis,* sed in plumbi natura molliti, [7] adhuc **operibus** servantes saeculo fidem, mentiri Deo per tonsuram noscuntur. [8] Qui bini aut terni aut certe singuli sine pastore, non dominicis sed suis inclusi ovilibus, pro lege eis est desideriorum voluntas, [9] cum quicquid putaverint vel elegerint, hoc dicunt sanctum, et quod noluerint, hoc putant non licere.

[10] Quartum vero genus est monachorum quod nominatur gyrovagum, qui tota vita sua per diversas provincias ternis aut quaternis diebus per diversorum cellas hospitantur, [11] **semper vagi et numquam stabiles, et propriis voluntatibus et gulae illecebris servientes, et per omnia deteriores sarabaitis.**

[12] **De quorum omnium horum miserrima conversatione melius est silere quam loqui.** [13] **His ergo omissis, ad coenobitarum fortissimum genus disponendum, adiuvante Domino, veniamus.**

(RM 2:1-10)

II QUALIS DEBEAT ESSE ABBAS

[1] Abbas qui praeesse dignus est monasterio semper meminere debet quod dicitur et nomen maioris factis implere. [2] Christi enim agere vices in monasterio creditur, quando ipsius vocatur pronomine, [3] dicente apostolo: *Accepistis spiritum adoptionis filiorum, in quo clmamus: abba, pater.*

[6] The third and most detestable kind of monks are the Sarabaites, who have neither been tried by a Rule nor taught by experience *like gold in the furnace;* (PROVERBS 27:21) instead they are as soft as lead, [7] faithful servants of the world **in their works**, obviously lying to God by their tonsure. [8] Living in twos or threes, or even singly without a shepherd, they enclose themselves not in the Lord's sheepfolds but in their own. Their law consists in their own wilful desires: [9] whatever they think fit or choose to do, that they call holy; and what they dislike, that they regard as unlawful.

[10] The fourth kind are the monks called gyrovagues, whose whole lives are spent in province after province, spending three or four days in monastery after monastery as guests: [11] **always wandering and never stable; slaves of self–will and the attractions of gluttony; in all things they are worse than the Sarabaites.**

[12] **Concerning all of these and their most miserable way of life it is better to remain silent than to speak.** [13] **Leaving them then, let us proceed with God's help to make provision for the Cenobites—the strong kind of monks.**

CHAPTER 2: QUALITIES THE ABBOT MUST HAVE

[1] An abbot who is worthy to govern a monastery must always remember what he is called and fulfill the name 'superior' in his deeds. [2] For it is Christ's place that he is believed to hold in the monastery, since he is addressed by His title, [3] as the Apostle said: *You have received the spirit of adoption of sons by which we cry,"Abba, Father"* (ROMANS 8:15).

[4] Ideoque abbas nihil extra praeceptum Domini quod sit debet aut docere aut constituere vel iubere, [5] **sed** iussio eius vel doctrina fermentum divinae iustitiae in discipulorum mentibus conspargatur, [6] memor semper abbas quia doctrinae suae vel discipulorum oboedientiae, **utrarumque** rerum, in tremendo iudicio Dei facienda erit discussio. [7] Sciat**que** abbas culpae pastoris incumbere quicquid in ovibus paterfamilias utilitatis minus potuerit invenire. [8] Tantundem iterum erit ut, si inquieto vel inoboedienti gregi pastoris fuerit omnis diligentia attributa et morbidis earum actibus universa fuerit cura exhibita, [9] pastor eorum in iudicio Domini absolutus dicat cum propheta Domino: *Iustitiam tuam non abscondi in corde meo, veritatem tuam et salutare tuum dixi; ipsi autem contemnentes spreverunt me*, [10] et tunc demum inoboedientibus curae suae ovibus poena sit eis praevalens ipsa mors.

(RM 2:23-25)

[11] Ergo, cum aliquis suscipit nomen abbatis, duplici debet doctrina suis praeesse discipulis, [12] id est omnia bona et sancta factis amplius quam verbis ostend**at**, **ut capacibus** discipulis mandata Domini verbis proponere, duris corde vero et simplicioribus factis suis divina praecepta monstrare. [13] Omnia vero quae discipulis docuerit esse contraria in suis factis indicet non agenda, *ne aliis pradicans ipse reprobus inceniatur,*

[4] Therefore the abbot should never teach or enact or command anything contrary to the precepts of the Lord; [5] **rather** his commands and his teaching, like the leaven of divine justice, are to suffuse the minds of his disciples. [6] The abbot is to remember always that his teaching and the obedience of his disciples— **both of these** matters—will be examined at the fearful judgment of God. [7] **And** the abbot must know that the shepherd will be considered at fault if the father of the household finds that the sheep bring no profit. [8] If, on the other hand, he has exercised all pastoral diligence over a restless and disobedient flock, always striving to heal their unhealthy ways; [9] then their shepherd will be absolved at the judgment of the Lord, and will say to the Lord with the prophet: *I have not hidden **your justice** in my heart; I have declared your truth and your salvation* (PSALM 40:11), *but they* condemned *and spurned me* (ISAIAH 1:2, EZEKIEL 20:27); [10] and then the sheep disobedient to his care will be punished by overpowering death.

Jan 11;   May 12;   Sept 11

[11] Therefore, when anyone receives the name of abbot he is to govern his disciples by a twofold teaching: [12] namely, all that is good and holy he must show forth more by deeds than by words; declaring **to receptive** disciples the commandments of the Lord in words, but to the hard-hearted and the simple-minded demonstrating the divine precepts by the example of his deeds. [13] And all of the things that he teaches his disciples are contrary [to the divine precepts]—his own deeds should indicate that these are not to be done, *lest while preaching to others, he himself be found reprobate* (I CORINTHIANS 9:27);

[14] ne quando illi *dicat Deus peccanti: Quare tu enarras iustitias meas et **adsumis** testamentum meum per os tuum? Tu vero odisti disciplinam **et proiecisti sermones meos post te**,* [15] et: *Qui in fratris tui oculo festucam videbas, in tuo trabem non vidisti.*

(RM 2:16-22)

[16] Non ab eo persona in monasterio discernatur. [17] Non unus plus ametur quam alius, nisi quem in bonis actibus **aut oboedientia** invenerit meliorem. [18] Non convertenti **ex** servitio praeponatur ingenuus, **nisi alia rationabilis causa exsistat.** [19] **Quod si ita, iustitia dictante, abbati visum fuerit, et de cuiuslibet ordine id faciet. Sin alias, propria teneant loca,** [20] quia *sive servus sive liber, omnes in Christo unum sumus* et sub uno Domino aequalem servitutis militiam baiulamus, quia *non est apud Deum personarum acceptio.*

[21] Solummodo in hac parte apud **ipsum** discernimur, si meliores ab aliis **in operibus bonis et humiles** inveniamur. [22] Ergo aequalis sit ab eo omnibus caritas, una praebeatur in omnibus **secundum merita** disciplina.

(RM 2:23-25)

[23] In doctrina sua namque abbas apostolicam debet illam semper formam servare in qua dicit: *Argue, obsecra, increpa,* [24] id est, miscens temporibus tempora, terroribus blandimenta, dirum magistri, pium patris ostendat affectum,

[14] and *God say* to him *in his sin: How can you recite my justice and declare my covenant with your mouth? For you hated discipline and cast my words behind you?* (PSALM 50:1-17) [15] And also: *How could you see a speck in your brother's eye, and not have noticed the plank in your own?* (MATTHEW 7:3)

Jan 12;   May 13;   Sept 12

[16] He is not to distinguish between persons in the monastery. [17] He should not love one more than another unless he finds him better in good deeds **or obedience.** [18] One born free is not to be put before one who enters religion from slavery, **except for some other reasonable cause.** [19] **Although, according to the dictates of justice, the abbot may see fit to change anyone's rank. Otherwise let each keep to his proper place,** [20] because *whether we are slaves or free, we are all one in Christ* (GALATIANS 3:28, EPHESIANS 6:8) and under one Lord serve equally in bearing arms: for *with God there is no partiality among persons* (ROMANS 2:11).

[21] Solely in this are we distinguished before **him**: if we are found better than others **in good works and humility.** [22] Therefore, let equal love be shown to all; and there should be imposed upon all, **according to their merits,** the same discipline.

Jan 13;   May 14;   Sept 13

[23] For in his teaching the abbot should always observe the Apostle's norm, where he says: *use argument, exhort, rebuke* (II TIMOTHY 4:2). [24] That is, he must adapt to circumstances, mingling gentleness with sternness, alternating the strictness of a master with the loving affection shown by a father:

[25] id est indisciplinatos et inquietos debet durius arguere, oboedientes autem et mites et patientes ut in melius proficiant obsecrare, neglegentes et contemnentes ut increpat et corripiat admonemus.

[26] **Neque dissimulet peccata delinquentium; sed et mox ut coeperint oriri radicitus ea ut praevalet amputet, memor periculi Heli sacerdotis de Silo.** [27] **Et honestiores quidem atque intellegibiles animos prima vel secunda admonitione verbis corripiat,** [28] **improbos autem et duros ac superbos vel inoboedientes verberum vel corporis castigatio in ipso initio peccati coerceat, sciens scriptum:** *Stultus verbis non corrigitur,* [29] **et iterum:** *Percute filium tuum virga et liberabis animam eius a morte.*

(RM 2:32)

[30] Meminere debet semper abbas quod est, meminere quod dicitur, et scire *quia cui* plus *committitur, plus ab eo* exigitur. [31] **Sciatque quam difficilem et arduam rem suscipit regere animas et multorum servire moribus, et alium quidem blandimentis, alium vero increpationibus, alium suasionibus;** [32] **et secundum uniuscuiusque qualitatem vel intellegentiam, ita se omnibus conformet et aptet ut non solum detrimenta gregis sibi commissi non patiatur, verum in augmentatione boni gregis gaudeat.**

[25] thus he should sternly argue with the undisciplined and restless; he will exhort the obedient, the mild, and the patient to advance in virtue; and the negligent and arrogant we admonish him to rebuke and correct.

[26] He must never disregard the sins of offenders; but as soon as they sprout, cut them out as best he can by the roots, remembering the fate of Eli, the priest of Shiloh. (I SAMUEL 2:11-4:18) **[27] Those of honorable and perceptive dispositions may for the first or second time be corrected with words of admonition; [28] but the shameless and hard, the arrogant or disobedient are to be checked by whipping or other corporal punishment at their first offense, knowing that it is written: *The fool is not corrected with words,* (PROVERBS 29:19) [29] and again, *Strike your son with a rod and you will free his soul from death* (PROVERBS 23:14).**

Jan 14; May 15; Sept 14

[30] The abbot must always remember what he is, remember what he is called, and know that *from him to whom more* is **committed***, more is required* (LUKE 12:48). [31] **And he must know how difficult and arduous is his received task of ruling souls and serving different temperaments: complimenting some, rebuking others, using persuasion with still others; [32] and according to the unique qualities and intelligence of each he must so conform and adapt himself that not only will the flock committed to him suffer no loss, but he will truly rejoice in the increase of a good flock.**

(RM 2:33-40)

³³ Ante omnia, ne dissimulans aut parvipendens salutem animarum sibi commissarum, ne plus gerat sollicitudinem de rebus transitoriis et terrenis atque caducis, ³⁴ sed semper cogitet quia animas suscepit regendas, de quibus et *rationem redditurus est.* ³⁵ Et ne causetur de minori forte substantia, meminerit scriptum: *Primum quaerite regnum Dei et iustitiam eius, et haec omnia adicientur vobis,* ³⁶ et iterum: *Nihil deest timentibus eum.* ³⁷ Sciatque quia qui suscipit animas regendas paret se ad rationem reddendam, ³⁸ et quantum sub cura sua fratrum se habere scierit numerum, agnoscat pro certo quia in die iudicii ipsarum omnium animarum est redditurus Domino rationem, sine dubio addita et suae animae. ³⁹ Et ita, timens semper futuram discussionem pastoris de creditis ovibus, cum de alienis ratiociniis cavet, redditur de suis sollicitus, ⁴⁰ et cum de monitionibus suis emendationem aliis sumministrat ipse efficitur a vitiis emendatus.

Jan 15; May 16; Sept 15

[33] **Above all he must not, by disregarding or undervaluing the salvation of the souls committed to him, be more solicitous for transitory, earthly, and perishable things;** [34] **rather let him always ponder that he who has received the ruling of souls *must render an account* of them** (*cf.* LUKE 16:2). [35] **And that he may not plead as his excuse a lack of resources, let him remember what is written: *Seek first the Kingdom of God and his justice, and all these things will be added unto you,*** (MATTHEW 6:33) [36] **and again: *Nothing is lacking to those who fear him.*** (PSALM 34:9) [37] **And he must know that he who has received the ruling of souls, must prepare himself to render an account of them:** [38] **and whatever the number of brothers under his care, he should know for certain that on the Day of Judgment he must render an account of all these souls to the Lord—and without doubt of his own soul as well.** [39] **And therefore, always fearful of the future judgment of the shepherd concerning the flock entrusted to him and thus carefully considerate of others, he will also be solicitous of what he must render that is his:** [40] **and so, in obtaining by his admonitions the amendment of others, he will also amend his own vices.**

(cf. RM 2:41-48)

III DE ADHIBENDIS AD CONSILIUM FRATRIBUS

[1] Quotiens aliqua praecipua agenda sunt in monasterio, convocet abbas omnem congregationem et dicat ipse unde agitur, [2] et audiens consilium fratrum tractet apud se et quod utilius iudicaverit faciat. [3] Ideo autem omnes ad consilium vocari diximus quia saepe iuniori Dominus revelat quod melius est. [4] Sic autem dent fratres consilium cum omni humilitatis subiectione, et non praesumant procaciter defendere quod eis visum fuerit, [5] et magis in abbatis pendat arbitrio, ut quod salubrius esse iudicaverit ei cuncti oboediant. [6] Sed sicut discipulos convenit oboedire magistro, ita et ipsum provide et iuste condecet cuncta disponere.

[7] In omnibus igitur omnes magistram sequantur regulam, neque ab ea temere declinetur a quoquam. [8] Nullus in monasterio proprii sequatur cordis voluntatem, [9] neque praesumat quisquam cum abbate suo proterve aut foris monasterium contendere. [10] Quod si praesumpserit, regulari disciplinae subiaceat. [11] Ipse tamen abbas cum timore Dei et observatione regulae omnia faciat, sciens se procul dubio de omnibus iudiciis suis aequissimo iudici Deo rationem redditurum.

Jan 16; May 17; Sept 16

CHAPTER 3: SUMMONING THE BROTHERS FOR COUNSEL

[1] Whenever anything important has to be done in the monastery, the abbot is to convoke the whole community, and himself declare the proposed action: [2] and having heard the counsel of the brethren, he is to ponder it over within himself and then do what he judges most appropriate. [3] Now, we have said that all should be called to council because it is often to the younger that the Lord reveals what is best. [4] But the brothers are to give their counsel with all the submissiveness of humility, and not presume insolently to defend their own views: [5] it is, rather, on the abbot's decision that the matter depends, so that when he has judged what is most beneficial, all may obey. [6] Yet, even as it is natural for disciples to obey their master, so it is appropriate for him to settle everything with foresight and justice.

Jan 17; May 18; Sept 17

[7] In everything, therefore, all are to follow the Rule as their master: from it no one at all should have the temerity to turn aside. [8] No one in the monastery may follow the will of his own heart, [9] nor may any presume to brashly contend with his abbot, whether within or outside the monastery. [10] But if he presumes to do so, let him be subjected to the discipline of the Rule. [11] Moreover, the abbot himself must do everything in the fear of God, observing the Rule, knowing that without any doubt an account of all his judgments must be rendered to that most impartial judge, God.

¹² Si qua vero minora agenda sunt in monasterii utilitatibus, seniorum tantum utatur consilio, ¹³ sicut scriptum est: *Omnia fac cum consilio et postfactum non paeniteberis.*

(RM 3:1-19)

IV QUAE SUNT INSTRUMENTA BONORUM OPERUM

¹ In primis *Dominum Deum diligere ex toto corde, tota anima, tota virtute;* ² deinde *proximum tamquam seipsum.* ³ Deinde *non occidere,* ⁴ *non adulterare,* ⁵ *non facere furtum,* ⁶ *non concupiscere,* ⁷ *non falsum testimonium dicere,* ⁸ honorare **omnes homines,** ⁹ et *quod sibi quis fieri non vult, alio ne faciat.* ¹⁰ *Abnegare semetipsum* **sibi** *ut sequatur Christum.* ¹¹ *Corpus castigare,* ¹² delicias **non amplecti,** ¹³ ieiunium amare. ¹⁴ Pauperes recreare, ¹⁵ *nudum vestire,* ¹⁶ *infirmum visitare,* ¹⁷ *mortuum* sepelire. ¹⁸ In tribulatione subvenire, ¹⁹ dolentem consolari.

(RM 3:22-47)

²⁰ Saeculi actibus se facere alienum, ²¹ nihil amori Christi praeponere. ²² Iram non perficere, ²³ iracundiae tempus non reservare. ²⁴ Dolum in corde non tenere, ²⁵ pacem falsam non dare. ²⁶ Caritatem non derelinquere. ²⁷ *Non iurare ne* forte *periuret,* ²⁸ veritatem ex corde et ore proferre.

[12] **If less important matters are to be done for the good of the monastery, he is to take counsel only with the seniors,** [13]**as it is written:** *Do all things with counsel, and you will not afterwards repent of it* (SIRACH 32:24).

Jan 18; May 19; Sept 18

CHAPTER 4: WHAT ARE THE INSTRUMENTS OF GOOD WORKS

[1] First of all *to love the* **Lord** *God with one's whole heart, whole soul,* **whole strength** (MATTHEW 22:37-39; MARK 12:30-31; LUKE 10:47). [2] Then, to love one's neighbor as oneself. [3] Then, *not to kill,* [4] *not to commit adultery,* [5] *not to engage in theft,* [6] *not to ardently desire* (ROMANS 13:9), [7] *not to give false testimony* (MATTHEW 19:18; MARK 10:19; LUKE 18:20), [8] *to honor* **all** (I PETER 2:17). [9] and *not do to another what one does not want done to* oneself (TOBIT 4:16; MATTHEW 7:12; LUKE 6:31). [10] To deny one's **own** self *in order to follow Christ* (MATTHEW 16:24; LUKE 9:23). [11] *To chastise the body* (I COR 9:27): [12] **not to embrace** delicacies; [13] to love fasting. [14] To give new life to the poor; [15] *to clothe the naked,* [16] *to visit the sick* (MATTHEW 25:36), [17] to bury the dead (*cf.* TOBIT 1:21,2:7-9). [18] To help in tribulation; [19] to console the sorrowful.

Jan 19; May 20; Sept 19

[20] To become a stranger to worldly behavior; [21] to prefer nothing to the love of Christ. [22] Not to carry out anger: [23] not to store up wrath, awaiting a time of revenge, [24] not to cling to deceit within the heart, [25] not to give a false greeting of peace, [26] not to turn away from love. [27] *Not to swear,* lest you *swear falsely* (MATTHEW 5:34 & 33); [28] to bring forth the truth from heart and mouth.

29 *Malum pro malo non reddere.* 30 Iniuriam non facere, sed et factas patienter sufferre. 31 *Inimicos diligere.* 32 *Maledicentes se non remaledicere, sed magis benedicere.* 33 *Persecutionem pro iustitia sustinere.*

34 *Non esse superbum,* 35 *non vinolentum,* 36 *non multum edacem,* 37 non somnulentum, 38 *non pigrum,* 39 *non murmuriosum,* 40 **non detractorem.**

41 Spem suam Deo committere. 42 Bonum aliquid in se cum viderit, Deo **adplicet, non sibi;** 43 malum vero **semper** a se factum **sciat** et sibi reput**et.**

(RM 3:50-67)

44 Diem iudicii timere, 45 gehennam expavescere, 46 vitam aeternam **omni concupiscentia** spiritali desiderare, 47 morte cotidie ante oculos suspectam habere. 48 Actus vitae suae omni hora custodire, 49 in **omni** loco **Deum** se respicere pro certo scire. 50 Cogitationes malas cordi suo advenientes mox *ad* Christum *allidere* **et seniori spiritali patefacere,** 51 Os suum a malo vel pravo eloquio custodire, 52 multum loqui non amare, 53 verba vana aut risui apta non loqui, 54 risum multum aut excussum non amare.

55 Lectiones sanctas libenter audire, 56 orationi frequenter incumbere, 57 mala sua praeterita cum lacrimis vel gemitu cotidie in oratione Deo confiteri, 58 de ipsis malis de cetero emendare.

29 *Not to return evil for evil* (I THESSALONIANS 5:15, I PETER 3:9). 30 Not to cause injury, but rather to bear it patiently. 31 *To love one's enemies* (MATTHEW 5:44; LUKE 6:27). 32 *Not to curse back those who curse one, but rather to bless them.* (I PETER 3:9; LUKE 6:28) 33 *To endure persecution for justice's sake* (MATTHEW 5:10).

34 *Not to be proud* (TITUS 1:7), 35 *nor given to wine* (TITUS 1:7, I TIMOTHY 3:3), 36 *not to be a glutton* (SIRACH 37:32), 37 *nor given to sleeping* (PROVERBS 20:13), 38 *nor lazy* (ROMANS 12:11), 39 *not given to murmuring* 40 *nor to speaking ill of others* (WISDOM 1:11).

41 To place one's hope in God (PSALM 72:28). 42 To **attribute** whatever good one sees in oneself to God, **not to oneself**; 43 but **always** to clearly **acknowledge** and take personal responsibility for the evil one does.

Jan 20; May 21; Sept 20

44 To fear the Day of Judgment: 45 to dread hell; 46 to desire eternal life with **all ardent yearning,** 47 to daily keep death before one's eyes. 48 To keep custody at every hour over the actions of one's life, 49 to know with certainty that God sees one in **every** place. 50 To instantly *hurl* the evil thoughts of one's heart *against* Christ (PSALM 136:9) **and to lay them open to one's spiritual father**; 51 to keep custody of one's mouth against depraved speech, 52 not to love excessive speaking, 53 not to speak words that are vain or apt to provoke laughter (*cf.* II TIMOTHY 2:16), 54 not to love frequent or raucous laughter. (*cf.* SIRACH 21:23)

55 To listen willingly to holy readings, 56 to prostrate frequently in prayer; 57 to daily confess one's past faults to God in prayer with tears and sighs, 58 to amend these faults for the future.

[59] *Desideria carnis non efficere,* [60] voluntatem propriam odire, [61] **praeceptis** abbatis **in omnibus** oboedire, **etiam si ipse aliter—quod absit!—agat,** memores illud dominicum praeceptum: *Quae dicunt facite, quae autem faciunt facere nolite.*

(RM 3:68-82; 2:52)

[62] Non velle dici sanctum antequam sit, sed prius esse quod verius dicatur. [63] Praecepta Dei factis cotidie adimplere, [64] castitatem amare, [65] nullum odire, [66]zelum non habere, [67] invidiam non exercere, [68]contentionem non amare, [69] **elationem fugere.** [70] **Et seniores venerare,** [71] **iuniores diligere.** [72] **In Christi amore pro inimicis orare;** [73] cum **discordante** ante solis occasum in **pacem** redire.

[74] Et Dei **misericordia** numquam desperare.

[75] Ecce haec **sunt instrumenta** artis spiritalis. [76] Quae cum fuerint a nobis die noctuque incessabiliter adimpleta et in die iudicii reconsignata, illa mercis nobis a Domino reconpens**abitur** quam **ipse** promisit: [77] *Quod oculus non vidit nec auris audivit, quae praeparavit Deus his qui diligunt illum.* [78] Officina vero ubi haec omnia diligenter operemur **claustra sunt** monasterii **et stabilitas in congregatione.**

[59] Not to gratify *the desires of the flesh* (GALATIANS 5:16): [60] to hate one's own will. [61] to obey the **precepts** of the abbot **in everything even if he should (may it never happen!) act otherwise, remembering that** precept of the Lord: *what they say, do; but what they do, do not* (MATTHEW 23:3).

Jan 21; May 22; Sept 21

[62] Not to wish to be called holy before one is so; but first to be holy, so as to be truly called so. [63] To daily fulfill in one's actions the precepts of God: [64] to love chastity; [65] to hate no–one; [66] not to have jealousy, [67] not to act out of envy, [68] not to love contention, [69] **to flee from conceit.** [70] **to reverence the seniors;** [71] **and to love the juniors.** [72] **In the love of Christ to pray for enemies;** [73] to make **peace** with **opponents** before the setting of the sun.

[74] And never to despair of the **mercy** of God.

[75] Behold, these **are the instruments** of the spiritual art. [76] If we employ them night and day without ceasing and on the Day of Judgment return them, then these will be the wages by which the Lord will recompense us, as he promised: [77] *What eye has not seen, nor ear heard, the Lord has prepared for those who love him* (I CORINTHIANS 2:9). [78] For the workshop in which we diligently use all these instruments **is the enclosure** of the monastery **and stability in the community.**

(RM 7:1-9, 47-51)

V DE OBOEDIENTIA

[1] Primus humilitatis gradus est oboedientia sine mora.
[2] Haec convenit his qui nihil sibi a Christo carius
aliquid existimant. [3] Propter servitium sanctum quod
professi sunt seu propter metum gehennae vel gloriam
vitae aeternae, [4] mox aliquid imperatum a maiore
fuerit, **ac si divinitus imperetur** moram pati nesciant
in **faciendo.** [5] De quibus Dominus dicit: *Obauditu
auris oboedivit mihi.* [6] Et item dicit doctoribus: *Qui
vos audit me audit.* [7] Ergo hi tales, relinquentes statim
quae sua sunt et voluntatem propriam deserentes,
[8] mox exoccupatis manibus et quod agebant
imperfectum relinquentes, vicino oboedientiae pede
iubentis vocem factis sequuntur, [9] et veluti uno
momento praedicta magistri iussio et perfecta discipuli
opera, in velocitate timoris Dei, ambae res communiter
citius explicantur.

[10] Quibus ad vitam aeternam **gradiendi** amor incumbit,
[11] ideo angustam viam arripiunt—**unde Dominus
dicit:** *Angusta via est quae ducit ad vitam*— [12] ut non
suuo arbitrio viventes vel desideriis suis et voluptatibus
oboedientes, sed ambulantes alieno iudicio et imperio,
in coenobiis degentes abbatem sibi praeesse desiderant.
[13] Sine dubio hi tales illam Domini imitantur
sententiam qua dicit: *Non veni facere voluntatem
meam, sed eius qui misit me.*

Jan 22; May 23; Sept 22

CHAPTER 5: OBEDIENCE

[1] The first step of humility is obedience without hesitation. [2] This comes naturally to those who esteem nothing as more beloved to them than Christ. [3] Whether on account of the holy service they have professed or because of the fear of hell, and the glory of eternal life, [4] as soon as anything is ordered by the superior, **it is as if it had been commanded by God himself**, and they cannot bear any hesitation in **doing it.** [5] Of these men the Lord says: *On hearing with his ear he has obeyed me* (PSALM 18:44). [6] And again he says to teachers: *he who hears you hears me* (LUKE 10:16). [7] Such as these, therefore, leaving immediately all that is theirs and forsaking their own wills [8] at once disengage their hands and leaving unfinished what they were doing, follow by their deeds with the eager step of obedience, the voice of him who commands: [9] and as it were in a single moment, the master's bidding and the disciple's completed work are both, in the swiftness of the fear of God, instantly achieved.

[10] Those whom love impels to **advance** on the way of eternal life— [11] these lay hold of the narrow way **of which the Lord says: *Narrow is the way which leads to life*** (MATTHEW 7:14): [12] so that by neither living according to their own wills, nor obeying their own desires and pleasures, they walk instead according to the judgment and command of another, living in community, and desiring to have an abbot govern them. [13] Without doubt such as these embody that saying of the Lord which reads: *I did not come to do my own will, but that of him who sent me* (JOHN 6:38).

31

(RM 7:67-74)

[14] Sed haec ipsa oboedientia tunc acceptabilis erit Deo et dulcis hominibus, si quod iubetur non trepide, non tarde, non tepide, aut cum murmurio vel cum responso nolentis efficiatur, [15] quia oboedientia quae maioribus praebetur Deo **exhibetur—ipse enim** dixit: *Qui vos audit me audit.* [16] Et cum bono animo a discipulis praeberi **oportet**, quia *hilarem datorem diligit Deus.* [17] Nam, cum malo animo si oboedit discipulus et non solum ore sed **etiam in corde** si **murmuraverit**, [18] **etiam si** impleat **iussionem**, tamen acceptum iam non erit Deo qui cor eius respicit murmurantem, [19] et pro tali facto nullam **consequitur gratiam; immo poenam murmurantium incurrit, si non cum satisfactione emendaverit.**

(RM 8:31-37; 9:51)

VI DE TACITURNITATE

[1] **Faciamus quod ait** propheta: *Dixi: Custodiam vias meas, ut non delinquam in lingua mea. Posui ori meo custodiam. Obmutui et humiliatus sum et silui a bonis.* [2] Hic ostendit propheta si a bonis eloquiis interdum propter taciturnitatem debet taceri, quanto magis a malis verbis propter poenam peccati debet cessari. [3] Ergo, quamvis de bonis et sanctis et aedificationum eloquiis, perfectis discipulis propter taciturnitatis gravitatem rara loquendi concedatur licentia,

Jan 23; May 24; Sept 23

[14] But this very obedience will be acceptable to God and sweet to men only if what is commanded is done, not fearfully, sluggishly, or lukewarmly, and neither with murmuring, nor with an answer showing unwillingness: [15] for the obedience offered to superiors is **given** to God, **just as He Himself** said: *He who hears you hears me* (LUKE 10:16). [16] And this obedience ought to be offered with good will, because *God loves a cheerful giver* (II CORINTHIANS 9:7). [17] For if the disciple obeys with ill will, and **murmurs** not only with his lips but also **in his heart,** [18] **even if** he **fulfills** the command he will not be acceptable to God, who sees the heart of the murmurer: [19] and from this **no favor will follow; rather he will incur the punishment due to murmurers, unless he amends by making satisfaction.**

Jan 24; May 25; Sept 24

CHAPTER 6: ON RESTRAINT IN SPEAKING

[1] **Let us do as** the prophet **says:** *I said, I will keep custody over my ways so I do not sin with my tongue: I have kept custody over my mouth. I became speechless, and was humbled, and kept silent concerning good things* (PSALM 39:1-3). [2] Here the prophet shows that if we ought to refrain even from good words for the sake of restraining speech, how much more ought we to abstain from evil words, on account of the punishment due to sin! [3] Therefore, on account of the importance of restraint in speech let permission to speak be seldom granted even to perfect disciples, even when their conversation is good and holy and edifying,

[4] quia **scriptum est**: *In multiloquio non effugies peccatum,* [5] et **alibi**: Mors et vita in *manibus linguae.* [6] Nam loqui et docere magistrum condecet, tacere et audire discipulum convenit.

[7] **Et ideo, si qua requirenda sunt a priore, cum omni humilitate et subiectione reverentiae requirantur.** [8] Scurrilitates vero vel verba otiosa et risum moventia aeterna clausura in omnibus locis damnamus et ad talia eloquia discipulum aperire os non permittimus.

(RM 10:1-4)

VII DE HUMILITATE

[1] Clamat nobis scriptura divina, fratres, dicens: *Omnis qui se exaltat humiliabitul, et qui se humiliat exaltabitur.* [2] Cum haec ergo dicit, ostendit nobis omnem exaltationem genus esse superbiae. [3] Quod se cavere propheta indicat dicens: *Domine, non est exaltatum cor meum, neque elati sunt oculi mei; neque ambulavi in magnis, neque in mirabilibus super me.* [4] Sed quid? *Si non humiliter sentiebam, si exaltavi animam meam? –sicut ablactatum super matrem suam, ita retribuis in animam meam.*

(RM 10:5-9)

[5] Unde, fratres, si summae humilitatis volumus culmen attingere, et ad exaltationem illam caelestem, ad quam per praesentis vitae humilitatem ascenditur, volumus velociter pervenire, [6] actibus nostris ascendentibus scala illa erigenda est quae in somnio Jacob apparuit, *per* quam ei *descendentes et ascendentes angeli* monstrabantur.

[4] for **it is written**: *In speaking much you cannot avoid sin* (PROVERBS 10:19); [5] and **elsewhere**: *Death and life are in the hands of the tongue* (PROVERBS 18:21). [6] For speaking and teaching befit the master: remaining silent and listening are proper for the disciple.

[7] **And therefore, if something is requested of a superior, let it be requested with all humility and reverent submission.** [8] But as for ridiculing or otiose words, which induce laughter, we permanently ban them in every place, neither do we permit a disciple to open his mouth in such discourse.

Jan 25; May 26; Sept 25

CHAPTER 7: HUMILITY

[1] The Holy Scripture cries out to us, brothers, saying: *Everyone who exalts himself shall be humbled, and he who humbles himself shall be exalted* (LUKE 14:11; 18:14). [2] Therefore, by saying this, it teaches us that all exaltation is a kind of pride, [3] against which the prophet indicates that he guards himself, saying: *Lord, my heart is not exalted nor are my eyes lifted up; nor have I walked in great things, nor in wonders above me* (PSALM 131:1). [4] And why? *What if I did not think humbly, but exalted my soul; then like a child weaned from its mother —so you would treat my soul* (PSALM 131:2).

Jan 26; May 27; Sept 26

[5] Therefore, brothers, if we wish to arrive at the highest point of humility, and speedily reach that heavenly exaltation to which we can only ascend by the humility of this present life, [6] we must by our ever-ascending actions erect a ladder like the one which Jacob beheld in his dream, by which the *angels* appeared to him *descending and ascending* (GENESIS 28:12).

⁷ Non aliud sine dubio descensus ille et ascensus a nobis intelligitur, nisi exaltatione descendere et humilitate ascendere. ⁸ Scala vero ipsa erecta nostra est vita in saeculo, quae humiliato corde a Domino erigatur ad caelum. ⁹ Latera enim ejus scalae **dicimus** nostrum esse corpus et animam, in qua latera diversos gradus humilitatis vel disciplinae evocatio divina ascendendos inseruit.

(RM 10:10-17, 19)

¹⁰ Primus itaque humilitatis gradus **est,** si *timorem Dei* sibi *ante oculos* semper ponens oblivionem omnino fugiat ¹¹ et semper sit memor omnia quae praecepit Deus, ut **qualiter** et contemnentes **Deum** gehenna de peccatis incendat, et vitam aeternam, qu**ae** timentibus Deum praepar**ata est,** animo suo semper evolvat. ¹² Et custodiens se omni hora a peccatis et vitiis, id est cogitationum, linguae, manuum, pedum, vel voluntatis propriae, sed et desideria carnis, ¹³ aestimet se **homo** de caelis a Deo respici omni hora et facta sua omni loco ab aspectu divinitatis videri, et ab angelis omni hora renuntiari.

¹⁴ Demonstrans nobis hoc propheta, cum in cogitationibus nostris ita Deum semper praesentem ostendit dicens: *Scrutans corda et renes Deus;* ¹⁵ et item: *Dominus novit cogitationes hominum;* ¹⁶ et item dicit: *Intellexisti cogitationes meas a longe;* ¹⁷ et: *Quia cogitatio hominis confitebitur tibi.* ¹⁸ Nam ut sollicitus sit **circa** cogitationes su**as** perversas, dicat semper utilis frater in corde **suo:** *Tunc ero immaculatus coram eo, si observavero me ab iniquitate mea.*

[7] Without doubt this descent and ascent can signify nothing else than that we descend by exaltation and ascend by humility. [8] And the ladder thus erected is our life in the world, which, if the heart is humbled, is lifted up by the Lord to heaven. [9] The sides of the same ladder we **assert** to be our body and soul, in which the call of God has placed various steps of humility or discipline, which we must ascend.

Jan 27; May 28; Sept 27

[10] The first step of humility, then, **is** that one always keeps *the fear of God before his eyes,* (PSALM 36:2) fleeing every kind of forgetfulness, [11] and that one is ever mindful of all God has commanded, unfolding within his soul **that** those who despise **God** will be consumed in hell for their sins, and that eternal life **has been** prepared for those who fear Him. [12] And keeping custody over himself at every hour from sin and vice of thought, tongue, eyes, hands, feet, of his own will or of fleshly desires, [13] let this **man** consider that he is regarded from heaven by God at every hour, and that his actions in every place are perceived in the Divine Vision and are reported to God by His angels at every hour.

[14] This the prophet demonstrates to us, when he shows that God is always present to our thoughts, saying: *God searches the heart and the loins* (PSALM 7:10); [15] and again, *The Lord knows the thoughts of men* (PSALM 94:11); [16] and he also says: *You have understood my thoughts from afar* (PSALM 139:3); [17] and, *The thought of a man shall confess to you* (PSALM 76:11). [18] Therefore, so as to be on guard **against** perverse thoughts let the virtuous brother always say in his heart, *Then shall I be without stain before him, if I have kept myself from my iniquity* (PSALM 18:24).

(RM 10:30-34)

[19] Voluntatem vero propriam ita facere prohibemur cum dicit Scriptura nobis: *Et a voluntatibus tuis avertere.* [20] Et item rogamus **Deum** in oratione, ut *fiat illius voluntas in* nobis. [21] Docemur ergo merito nostram non facere voluntatem cum cavemus illud quod dicit sancta scriptura: *Sunt viae quae videntur ab hominibus rectae, quarum finis usque ad profundum inferni demergit;* [22] et cum item pavemus illud quod de negligentibus dictum est: *Corrupti sunt et abominabiles facti sunt in voluptatibus suis.* [23] In desideriis vero carnis ita nobis Deum cred**amus** semper esse praesentem, cum dicit propheta Domino: *Ante te est omne desiderium meum.*

(RM 10:35-41)

[24] Cavendum ergo ideo malum desiderium, quia *mors secus introitum delectationis posita est.* [25] Unde Scriptura praecipit dicens: *Post concupiscentias tuas non eas.*

[26] Ergo, *si oculi Domini speculantur bonos et malos,* [27] et *Dominus de caelo semper respicit super filios hominum, ut videat si est intelligens aut requirens Deum;* [28] et si ab angelis nobis deputatis cotidie die noctuque Domino factorum nostrorum opera nuntiantur, [29] cavendum est ergo omni hora, fratres, sicut dicit in psalmo propheta, ne nos *declinantes* in malo et *inutiles factos* aliqua hora aspiciat **Deus** [30] et, parcendo nobis in hoc tempore, quia pius est et exspectat nos converti in melius, **ne** dicat nobis in futuro: *Haec fecisti et tacui.*

¹⁹ For it is truly our own will that we are forbidden to do as Scripture tells us: *and turn away from your own will* (SIRACH 18:30). ²⁰ And so too we request of **God** in the prayer that His will may be done in us. ²¹ Thus we are rightly taught not to do our will, being warned as Sacred Scripture says that *there are ways which appear right to men, but which at their end plunge into the depths of hell* (PROVERBS 16:25); ²² or again, when we shudder at what is said of the negligent: *They are corrupt and have become abominable in their pleasures* (PSALM 14:1). ²³ Truly, as regards the desires of the flesh we believe that God is always present to us, as the prophet says to the Lord: *Before you is all my desire* (PSALM 38:10).

²⁴ Let us be on our guard then against evil desires, since death has its seat close to the entrance of delight. ²⁵ Hence the precept of Scripture, where it says: *Do not go after your desires* (SIRACH 18:30).

²⁶ Therefore, if *the eyes of the Lord behold the good and the evil* (PROVERBS 15:3); ²⁷ and the *Lord is always looking down from heaven on the children of men to see whether anyone has understanding or seeks God* (PSALM 14:2); ²⁸ and if the angels deputed to us report to the Lord every day, both by day and night, concerning the works we accomplish, ²⁹ then we must be on our guard at every hour, brothers, lest as the prophet says in the psalm, **God** should see us at any hour *inclining* to evil and *becoming useless* (PSALM 14:3); ³⁰ and lest, despite sparing us now because He is loving and expects our conversion and improvement, He should say to us in the future: *This you did and I was silent* (PSALM 49:21).

(RM 10:42-44)

[31] Secundus humilitatis gradus **est,** si propriam **quis** non amans voluntatem desideria sua non delectetur implere, [32] sed vocem illam Domini factis imitetur dicentis: *Non veni facere voluntatem meam, sed ejus qui me misit.* [33] Item dicit scriptura: *Voluptas habet poenam, et necessitas parit coronam.*

(RM 10:45, 49)

[34] Tertius humilitatis gradus **est, ut quis pro Dei amore** omni obedientia se subdat majori, imitans Dominum de quo dicit apostolus: *Factus obediens usque ad mortem.*

(RM 10:52-60)

[35] Quartus humilitatis gradus **est,** si in ipsa obedientia, duris et contrariis rebus vel etiam quibuslibet irrogatis injuriis, tacita **conscientia** patienti**am** amplectatur, [36] et sustinens non lassescat vel discedat, dicente Scriptura: *Qui perseveraverit usque in finem, hic salvus erit;* [37] Item: *Confortetur cor tuum, et sustine Dominum.* [38] Et ostendens fidelem pro Domino universa etiam contraria sustinere debere, dicit ex persona sufferentium: *Propter te morte afficimur tota die; aestimati sumus ut oves occisionis.* [39] Et securi de spe retributionis divinae subsequuntur gaudentes et dicentes: *Sed in his omnibus superamus propter eum qui dilexit nos.*

31 The second step of humility **is** that one does not love his own will, nor delight in satisfying his own desires, 32 but imitates in his deeds that saying of the Lord: *I did not come to do my own will, but that of him who sent me* (JOHN 6:38). 33 And again Scripture says: *Gratification deserves punishment, but necessity wins a crown (THE PASSION OF ANASTASIA 17).*

34 The third step of humility **is that for the love of God** one submits himself in all obedience to his superior, imitating the Lord of whom the apostle says: *He was made obedient even unto death* (PHILIPPIANS 2:8).

35 The fourth step of humility **is** that if in the exercise of this very obedience hard and contrary things, even injustices, are done to one, he embraces patience silently in his **conscience,** 36 and in enduring does not weaken or give up, as Scripture says: *He who perseveres to the end will be saved* (MATTHEW 10:22); 37 and again, *Let your heart take comfort, and rely on the Lord* (PSALM 27:14). 38 And showing that the faithful ought to bear everything for the Lord, however contrary, this text is placed in the mouth of the one who suffers: *For you we are afflicted with death the whole day; we are esteemed as sheep to be slaughtered* (ROMANS 8:36; PSALM 44:22). 39 And secure in the hope of divine reward they go forward, rejoicing and saying: *But in all these things we are triumphant, because of Him who has loved us* (ROMANS 8:37).

[40] Et item alio loco Scriptura: *Probasti nos, Deus, igne nos examinasti, sicut igne examinatur argentum: induxisti nos in laqueo; posuisti tribulationes in dorso nostro.* [41] Et ut ostendat sub **priore** debere nos esse, subsequitur dicens: *Imposuisti homines super capita nostra.*

[42] Sed et praeceptum Domini in adversis et injuriis per patientiam adimplentes, *qui percussi in maxillam praebent et aliam,* **auferenti** *tunicam dimittunt et pallium, angariati miliario vadunt duo,* [43] cum Paulo Apostolo *falsos fratres* sustinent, *et persecutionem* **sustinent** *et maledicentes se benedicent.*

(RM 10:61-65)

[44] Quintus humilitatis gradus **est,** si omnes cogitationes malas cordi suo advenientes, vel mala a se absconse commissa, per humilem confessionem abbatem non celaverit suum. [45] Hortans nos de hac re Scriptura dicens: *Revela ad Dominum viam tuam et spera in eum.* [46] Et item dicit: *Confitemini Domino, quoniam bonus, quoniam in saeculum misericordia ejus.* [47] Et item propheta: *Delictum meum cognitum tibi feci, et injustitias meas non operui.* [48] *Dixi, pronuntiabo* **adversum** *me injustitias meas Domino, et tu remisisti impietatem cordis mei.*

40 And also in another place Scripture says: *You have tested us, O God; with fire as silver is tested with fire; you have led us into the trap and laid tribulation on our backs* (PSALM 66:10-11). 41 And in order to show that we should be under a **superior** it continues, saying: *You have imposed men over our heads* (PSALM 66:12).

42 Indeed, they are fulfilling the precept of the Lord by patience in adversities and injuries who, *when struck on one cheek offer the other; to him who **takes away** their tunic they give their cloak; and when required to go one mile, they go two* (MATTHEW 5:39-41): 43 with Paul the Apostle they bear *false brothers, bear persecutions,* and *bless those who curse them* (II CORINTHIANS 11:26; I CORINTHIANS 4:12).

Feb 2; June 3; Oct 3

44 The fifth step of humility **is** when through humble confession one does not hide from one's abbot the evil thoughts that enter one's heart, nor the evils committed in secret. 45 Exhorting us in this regard Scripture says, *Make known to the Lord your way and hope in Him* (PSALM 37:5). 46 And again it says: *Confess to the Lord, for He is good; for His mercy is for all ages* (PSALM 106:1; PSALM 118:1). 47 And again the prophet says: *My offense I have made known to You, and my injustices I have not hidden.* 48 *I said, I will accuse myself before the Lord of my unjust deeds, and You have forgiven the disloyalty of my heart* (PSALM 32:5).

(RM 10:66-67)

[49] Sextus humilitatis gradus **est,** si omni vilitate vel extremitate contentus sit **monachus,** et ad omnia quae sibi **iniunguntur** velut operarium se malum judicet et indignum, [50] dicens sibi cum propheta: *Ad nihilum redactus sum et nescivi; ut jumentum factus sum apud te, et ego semper tecum.*

(RM 10:68-71)

[51] Septimus humilitatis gra**dus est,** si omnibus se inferiorem et viliorem non solum sua lingua pronuntiet, sed etiam intimo cordis credat affectu, [52] humilians se et dicens **cum propheta:** *Ego autem sum vermis et non homo, opprobrium hominum et abjectio plebis.* [53] *Exaltatus sum et humiliatus et confusus.* [54] Et item: *Bonum mihi quod humiliasti me,ut discam mandata tua.*

(RM 10:72)

[55] Octavus humilitatis gradus **est,** si nihil agat **monachus** nisi quod communis monasterii regula vel maiorum cohortantur exempla.

(RM 10:75-77)

[56] Nonus humilitatis gradus **est,** *si linguam* ad loquendum pro*hibeat* **monachus,** et taciturnitatem habens usque ad interrogationem non loquatur, [57] monstrante Scriptura quia *in multiloquio non effugitur peccatum;* [58] et quia vir *linguosus non* dirig*itur super terram.*

Feb 3; June 4; Oct 4

[49] The sixth step of humility is that a **monk** should be content with the most common and worst of everything, and in all that is **required** of him to judge himself a bad and worthless worker, [50] saying of himself with the prophet: *I was reduced to nothing and did not realize it; I have become like a beast before you, yet I am always with you* (PSALM 73:22-23).

Feb 4; June 5; Oct 5

[51] The seventh step of humility **is** that he should not only pronounce with his tongue that he is inferior to and more common than all, but also believe it in the intimate sensibility of his heart, [52] humbling himself and saying **with the prophet:** *As for me, I am a worm and no man, shameful among men and an outcast of the people* (PSALM 22:7). [53] *I have been exalted, and cast down and confounded* (PSALM 88:16). [54] And again: *It is good for me that you have humbled me, that I may learn your commandments* (PSALM 119:71,73).

Feb 5; June 6; Oct 6

[55] The eighth step of humility **is** for a **monk** to do nothing except what is encouraged by the common rule of the monastery or the example of the superiors.

Feb 6; June 7; Oct 7

[56] The ninth step of humility **is** that a **monk** *prohibit his tongue* from speaking (PSALM 34:14), having restraint of speech unless asked a question, [57] for Scripture makes clear that *In speaking much you cannot avoid sin* (PROVERBS 10;19) [58] and, *The talkative man is without direction on earth* (PSALM 140:12).

(RM 10:78)

59 Decimus humilitatis gradus **est,** si non sit facilis ac promptus in risu, quia scriptum est: *Stultus in risu exaltat vocem suam.*

(RM 10:80-81)

60 Undecimus humilitatis gradus **est,** si cum loquitur **monachus,** leniter et sine risu, humiliter cum gravitate, vel pauca verba et **rationabilia** loquatur, et non sit clamosus in voce; 61 sicut scriptum est: *Sapiens verbis innotescit paucis.*

(RM 10:82-91)

62 Duodecimus humilitatis gradus **est** si non solum corde **monachus,** sed etiam ipso corpore humilitatem videntibus se semper indicet; 63 id est, in opere Dei, in oratorio, in monasterio, in horto, in via, in agro, vel ubicumque, sedens, ambulans vel stans, inclinato **sit** semper capite, defixis in ter**ram** aspectibus, 64 reum se omni hora de peccatis suis aestimans, jam se tremendo judicio repraesentari aestimet; 65 dicens sibi in corde semper illud quod publicanus **ille evangelicus** fixis in terram oculis dixit: *Domine, non sum dignus, ego peccator levare oculos meos ad caelos;* 66 et item cum propheta: *Incurvatus sum et humiliatus sum usquequaque.*

59 The tenth step of humility **is** that one is not easily or promptly moved to laughter, for it is written: *The fool raises his voice in laughter* (SIRACH 21:23).

60 The eleventh step of humility **is** that when speaking the **monk** does so gently and without laughter, humbly and with gravity, speaking few but **reasonable** words, and that his voice is not clamorous: 61 as it is written, *A wise man is known by his few words.* (*THE SENTENCES OF SEXTUS* 145)

62 The twelfth step of humility **is** that the **monk,** not only in his heart, but by means of his own body always indicates his humility to those who see him 63—that is, at the Work of God, in the oratory, in the monastery, in the garden, on the road, in the field, or wherever he may be, whether sitting, walking, or standing—with head always inclined and gaze fixed on the ground, 64 estimating at every hour his sins, he should estimate himself as present at the terrible judgment, 65 saying always in his heart what the publican **in the Gospel** said with eyes fixed on the earth: *Lord, I am not worthy, sinner that I am, to lift my eyes up to heaven* (LUKE 18:13); 66 and again, with the prophet: *I am bent down and humbled in every way* (PSALM 38:7-9; PSALM 119:107).

[67] Ergo his omnibus humilitatis gradibus ascensis, **monachus** mox *ad caritatem* **Dei** perveniet illam quae *perfecta foris mittit timorem,* [68] per quam universa quae prius non sine formidine observabat, absque ullo labore velut naturaliter ex consuetudine incipiet custodire, [69] non iam timore gehennae sed amore **Christi,** et consuetudine ipsa bona et delectatione virtutum. [70] Quae Dominus iam in operarium suum mundum a vitiis et peccatis Spiritu Sancto dignabitur demonstrare.

(RM 33:3, 10 15-21,35; 44:12-14)

VIII DE OFFICIIS DIVINIS IN NOCTIBUS

[1] Hiemis tempore, **id est a** kalendas **Novembres usque in Pascha, iuxta considerationem rationis, octava hora noctis** surgendum est, [2] **ut modice amplius de media nocte pausetur et iam** digesti **surgant.** [3] **Quod vero restat post vigilias a** fratribus **qui psalterii vel** lectionum **aliquid indigent** meditationi inserviatur.

[4] A Pascha autem usque **ad supradictas Novembres, sic temperetur hora ut vigiliarum agenda parvissimo intervallo, quo fratres ad necessaria naturae exeant, mox matutini, qui incipiente luce agendi sunt, subsequantur.**

⁶⁷ Having therefore ascended all these steps of humility, the **monk** will soon arrive *at that love* **of God** which, being *perfect, casts out fear* (I JOHN 4:18): ⁶⁸ whereby all that he formerly observed not without dread, he will begin to keep without effort, as if naturally, out of habit; ⁶⁹ no longer from fear of hell but for the love of **Christ,** from good habit and delight in virtue. ⁷⁰ This God through the Holy Spirit will now grant his laborer to manifest, cleansed from vices and sins.

Feb 10; June 11; Oct 11

CHAPTER 8: THE DIVINE OFFICE AT NIGHT

¹ In the winter season, **that is from November** first **until Easter, we consider it reasonable to arise at the eighth hour of the night,** ² **so that having rested a little past midnight they may** arise **with their** food **fully** digested. ³ **The time that remains after Vigils should be spent in meditation by those** brothers **who still need to memorize some part of the** psalter **or** readings.

⁴ From Easter to the **aforementioned first of November the hour of Vigils should be so arranged that after a very short interval, during which the brothers may go out for the necessities of nature, Lauds (which are to begin at first light) may follow without delay.**

(RM 32:12-13; 42:1-8)

IX QUANTI PSALMI DICENDI SUNT NOCTURNIS HORIS

[1] Hiemis tempore suprascripto, in primis versu tertio dicendum: *Domine, labia mea aperies, et os meum adnuntiabit laudem tuam.* [2] Cui subiungendus est tertius psalmus et gloria. [3] Post hunc, psalmum nonagesimum quartum cum antiphona, aut certe decantandum. [4] Inde sequatur ambrosianum, deinde sex psalmi cum antiphonas.

[5] Quibus dictis, dicto versu, benedicat abbas et, sedentibus omnibus in scamnis, legantur vicissim a fratribus in codice super analogium tres lectiones, inter quas et tria responsoria cantentur: [6] duo responsoria sine gloria dicantur; post tertiam vero lectionem, qui cantat dicat gloriam. [7] Quam dum incipit cantor dicere, mox omnes de sedilia sua surgant, ob honorem et reverentiam sanctae Trinitatis. [8] Codices autem legantur in vigiliis divinae auctoritatis, tam veteris testamenti quam novi, sed et expositiones earum, quae a nominatis et orthodoxis catholicis patribus factae sunt.

[9] Post has vero tres lectiones cum responsoria sua, sequantur reliqui sex psalmi, cum alleluia canendi. [10] Post hos, lectio apostoli sequatur, ex corde recitanda, et versus, et supplicatio litaniae, id est *Kyrie eleison.* [11] Et sic finiantur vigiliae nocturnae.

CHAPTER 9: HOW MANY PSALMS ARE SAID AT THE NIGHT HOURS

[1] In winter time the aforementioned [Vigil] begins with this verse, repeated three times: *O Lord, open my lips; and my mouth shall announce your praise* (PSALM 51:16). [2] Then comes Psalm Three with a 'Glory be;' [3] then Psalm Ninety–four with a refrain, or at least chanted. [4] After that follws an Ambrosian hymn, then six psalms with refrains.

[5] These being sung, a versicle is read and the abbot gives the blessing. All being seated in their places, the brothers read in turn three lessons from the book on the lectern; three responsories are sung between the readings— [6] two of them without a 'Glory be,' but after the third the cantor is to intone a 'Glory be,' [7] all the monks rising from their places out of honor and reverence for the Holy Trinity. [8] The books to be read at Vigils are those of divine authority, both the Old and New Testaments are to be read at Vigils, as well as expositions of them by the most renowned and orthodox catholic fathers.

[9] After these three lessons with their responsories six more psalms follow with a sung 'alleluia.' [10] After this a reading from the apostle follows, recited by heart, and a verse, and the litany of supplication—that is, the 'Lord, have mercy.' [11] And thus the Vigils of the night come to an end.

(RM 33:35-41; 44:5-8)

X QUALITER AESTATIS TEMPORE AGATUR NOCTURNA LAUS

[1] A Pascha autem usque ad kalendas Novembres, omnis ut supra dictum est psalmodiae quantitas teneatur, [2] excepto quod lectiones in codice, propter brevitatem noctium, minime legantur, sed pro ipsis tribus lectionibus una de veteri testamento memoriter dicatur, quam brevis responsorius subsequatur. [3] Et reliqua omnia ut dictum est impleantur, id est ut numquam minus a duodecim psalmorum quantitate ad vigilias nocturnas dicantur, exceptis tertio et nonagesimo quarto psalmo.

(RM *cf.* 49:1-3; 44:5-8)

XI QUALITER DIEBIUS DOMINICIS VIGILIAE AGANTUR

[1] Dominico die temperius surgatur ad vigilias. [2] In quibus vigiliis teneatur mensura, id est, modulatis ut supra disposuimus sex psalmis et versu, residentibus cunctis disposite et per ordinem in subselliis, legantur in codice, ut supra diximus, quattuor lectiones cum responsoriis suis. [3] Ubi tantum in quarto responsorio dicatur a cantante gloria; quam dum incipit, mox omnes cum reverentia surgant.

[4] Post quibus lectionibus sequantur ex ordine alii sex psalmi cum antiphonas sicut anteriores, et versu. [5] Post quibus iterum legantur aliae quattuor lectiones cum responsoriis suis, ordine quo supra.

Feb 12; June 13; Oct 13

CHAPTER 10: HOW THE NIGHT OFFICE IS TO BE CELEBRATED IN SUMMER

[1] From Easter to the first of November, the same number of psalms is to be maintained as described above, [2] except that no lessons are to be read from the book on account of the brevity of the nights; instead of those three lessons, one from the Old Testament is said by heart, followed by a short responsory. [3] And all that remains is as described above: that is, there are never said fewer than twelve psalms at the nocturnal vigil, not counting Psalms Three and Ninety–four.

Feb 13; June 14; Oct 14

CHAPTER 11: HOW VIGILS ARE CELEBRATED ON SUNDAY

[1] On Sundays the brethren are to arise earlier for Vigils. [2] At these Vigils they are to keep to the same measure: that is, as prescribed above, having sung six psalms and a versicle all are to be seated on benches in their proper order, and four lessons with their responsories are read from the book, as described above. [3] But only after the fourth responsory does the cantor intone a 'Glory be', all standing in reverence as he begins it.

[4] After these lessons there follow according to the same pattern six more psalms with their refrains and versicles as above. [5] After this there are again read four more lessons with their responsories, according to the pattern above.

6 Post quibus dicantur tria cantica de prophetarum, quas instituerit abbas; quae cantica cum alleluia psallantur. 7 Dicto etiam versu et benedicente abbate, legantur aliae quattuor lectiones de novo testamento, ordine quo supra. 8 Post quartum autem responsorium incipiat abbas hymnum *Te Deum laudamus*. 9 Quo perdicto, legat abbas lectionem de Evangelia, cum honore et timore stantibus omnibus. 10 Qua perlecta, respondeant omnes Amen, et subsequatur mox abbas hymnum *Te decet laus*, et data benedictione incipiant matutinos.

11 Qui ordo vigiliarum omni tempore tam aestatis quam hiemis aequaliter in die dominico teneatur. 12 Nisi forte—quod absit—tardius surgant: aliquid de lectionibus breviandum est, aut responsoriis. 13 Quod tamen omnino caveatur ne proveniat. Quod si contigerit, digne inde satisfaciat Deo in oratorio per cuius evenerit neglectum.

(RM 35:1; 39:2-7)

XII QUOMODO MATUTINORUM SOLLEMNITAS AGATUR

1 In matutinis dominico die, in primis dicatur sexagesimus sextus psalmus, sine antiphona, in directum. 2 Post quem dicatur quinquagesimus cum alleluia. 3 Post quem dicatur centesimus septimus decimus et sexagesimus secundus. 4 Inde benedictiones et laudes, lectionem de Apocalypsis una ex corde, et responsorium, ambrosianum, versu, canticum de Evangelia, litania, et completum est.

⁶ After this, three canticles from the prophets are said, as the abbot directs, these canticles being sung with an 'alleluia.' ⁷ After the versicle and the abbot's blessing, four lessons from the New Testament are read as above. ⁸ But after the fourth responsory the abbot begins the hymn 'We praise you, O God.' ⁹ That having been sung, the abbot reads the lesson from the Gospel while all stand in honor and fear. ¹⁰ This having been read, all respond 'Amen,' following which the abbot immediately begins the hymn 'To you be praise,' and after the blessing is given Lauds begins.

¹¹ This order for Vigils should be kept on Sundays at all times, equally in summer and in winter, ¹² That is, unless (may it never happen!) they arise too late: in this case the readings or responsories may be somewhat shortened. ¹³ But all caution should be exercised so that this does not happen. However, if it does occur the one through whose neglect it has come to pass must make fitting satisfaction for it to God in the oratory.

Feb 14; June 15; Oct 15

CHAPTER 12: HOW THE SOLEMN OFFICE OF LAUDS IS TO BE CELEBRATED

¹ At Lauds on Sunday Psalm Sixty–six is first sung straight through without a refrain. ² After this, Psalm Fifty is sung with 'alleluia.' ³ Then Psalms One hundred and seventeen and sixty–two are sung. ⁴ After this follows the *Blessed are You* [CANTICLE OF THE THREE YOUNG MEN], the *Praises* [PSALMS 148-150], a lesson from the Apocalypse said by heart, a responsory, an Ambrosian hymn, a versicle, a canticle from the Gospel, the litany; and so it is completed.

(RM 35:1; 39:2-7)

XIII PRIVATIS DIEBUS QUALITER AGANTUR MATUTINI

[1] Diebus autem privatis, matutinorum sollemnitas ita agatur, [2] id est, ut sexagesimus sextus psalmus dicatur sine antiphona, subtrahendo modice, sicut dominica, ut omnes occurrant ad quinquagesimum, qui cum antiphona dicatur. [3] Post quem alii duo psalmi dicantur secundum consuetudinem, id est: [4] secunda feria, quintum et tricesimum quintum; [5] tertia feria, quadragesimum secundum et quinquagesimum sextum; [6] quarta feria, sexagesimum tertium et sexagesimum quartum; [7] quinta feria, octogesimum septimum et octogesimum nonum; [8] sexta feria, septuagesimum quintum et nonagesimum primum; [9] sabbatorum autem, centesimum quadragesimum secundum et canticum Deuteronomium qui dividatur in duas glorias. [10] Nam ceteris diebus canticum unumquemque die suo ex prophetis sicut psallit ecclesia Romana dicatur. [11] Post haec sequantur laudes; deinde lectio una apostoli memoriter recitanda, responsorium, ambrosianum, versu, canticum de Evangelia, litania et completum est.

[12] Plane agenda matutina vel vespertina non transeat aliquando nisi in ultimo per ordinem oratio dominica, omnibus audientibus, dicatur a priore, propter scandalorum spinas quae oriri solent, [13] ut conventi per ipsius orationis sponsionem qua dicunt: *Dimitte nobis sicut et nos dimittimus*, purgent se ab huiusmodi vitio. [14] Ceteris vero agendis, ultima pars eius orationis dicatur, ut ab omnibus respondeatur: *Sed libera nos a malo*.

Feb 15; June 16; Oct 16

CHAPTER 13: HOW LAUDS ARE CELEBRATED ON ORDINARY WEEKDAYS

[1] On ordinary weekdays, Lauds is to be performed as follows: [2] Psalm Sixty–six is sung without a refrain and somewhat slowly as on Sunday, so that all may be in time for Psalm Fifty, which is to be sung with a refrain. [3] After this two more psalms are sung according to custom, that is: [4] on Monday, Psalms Five and Thirty–five;[5] on Tuesday, Psalms Forty–two and Fifty–six; [6] on Wednesday, Psalms Sixty–three and Sixty–four; [7] on Thursday, Psalms Eighty–seven and Eighty–nine; [8] on Friday, Psalms Seventy–five and Ninety–one; [9] on Saturday, Psalm One hundred and forty–two and the canticle from Deuteronomy, which is to be divided with two 'Glory be.' [10] But on other days canticles from the prophets are said, according to the psalmody of the Roman Church. [11]After this should follow the 'Praises' [PSALMS 148-150], a lesson from the Apostle recited from memory, a responsory, an Ambrosian hymn, a versicle, the canticle from the Gospel; and with the litany it is completed.

Feb 16; June 17; Oct 17

[12] Most certainly the celebration of Lauds and Vespers should never pass by without the Lord's Prayer said aloud at the end by the Superior for all to hear, because of the thorns of scandal which are likely to spring up: [13] so that the brothers, by means of the promise they make in that prayer which says *Forgive us as we forgive* (MATTHEW 6:12), may purge themselves of this sort of vice. [14] But at the other offices, only the last part of this prayer is sung aloud, so that the response may be offered by all: *But deliver us from evil* (MATTHEW 6:13).

XIV IN NATALICIIS SANCTORUM QUALITER AGANTUR VIGILIAE

[1] In sanctorum vero festivitatibus, vel omnibus sollemnitatibus, sicut diximus dominico die agendum, ita agatur, [2] excepto quod psalmi aut antiphonae vel lectiones ad ipsum diem pertinentes dicantur; modus autem suprascriptus teneatur.

(RM 45:1, 12)

XV ALLELUIA QUIBUS TEMPORIBUS DICATUR

[1] A sanctum Pascha usque Pentecosten, sine intermissione dicatur alleluia, tam in psalmis quam in responsoriis. [2] A Pentecosten autem usque caput quadragesimae, omnibus noctibus, cum sex posterioribus psalmis tantum ad nocturnos dicatur. [3] Omni vero dominica extra quadragesima, cantica, matutinos, prima, tertia, sexta nonaque cum alleluia dicatur, vespera vero iam antiphona. [4] Responsoria vero numquam dicantur cum alleluia, nisi a Pascha usque Pentecosten.

Feb 17; June 18; Oct 18

CHAPTER 14: HOW VIGILS ARE CELEBRATED ON SAINT'S DAYS

[1] The feasts of saints and all solemnities should be celebrated as was described for the celebration on Sundays, [2] except that the psalms, refrains and readings pertaining to that day are used; otherwise the form described above is to be adhered to.

Feb 18; June 19; Oct 19

CHAPTER 15: AT WHAT TIMES 'ALLELUIA' IS SAID

[1] From holy Easter until Pentecost, without interruption, 'alleluia' is said both with the psalms and the responsories. [2] From Pentecost until the beginning of Lent, it is to be said every night, only with the second six psalms of Vigils. [3] On every Sunday outside Lent, the canticles, Vigils, Lauds, Prime, Terce, Sext and None are said with 'alleluia', but at Vespers a refrain is used. [4] Responsories, however, are never to be said with 'alleluia', except from Easter to Pentecost.

(RM 34:1-3; 33:1)

XVI QUALITER DIVINA OPERA PER DIEM AGANTUR

[1] Ut ait propheta, *septies in die laudem dixi tibi.*
[2] Qui septenarius sacratus numerus a nobis sic
implebitur, si matutino, primae, tertiae, sextae, nonae,
vesperae completoriique tempore nostrae servitutis
officia persolvamus, [3] quia de his diurnis horis dixit:
Septies in die laudem dixi tibi. [4] Nam de nocturnis
vigiliis idem ipse propheta ait: *Media nocte surgebam
ad confitendum tibi.* [5] Ergo his temporibus referamus
laudes Creatori nostro super iudicia iustitiae suae,
id est matutinis, prima, tertia, sexta, nona, vespera,
completorios, et nocte surgamus ad confitendum ei.

(RM 48:3)

XVII QUOT PSALMI PER EASDEM HORAS CANENDI SUNT

[1] Iam de nocturnis vel matutinis digessimus
ordinem psalmodiae; nunc de sequentibus horis
videamus.

[2] Prima hora dicantur psalmi tres singillatim et non
sub una gloria, [3] hymnum eiusdem horae post
versum *Deus in adiutorium* antequam psalmi
incipiantur. [4] Post expletionem vero trium
psalmorum recitetur lectio una, versu et Kyrie
eleison et missas.

CHAPTER 16: HOW THE WORK OF GOD IS TO BE CELEBRATED DURING THE DAY

[1] As the Prophet says: *Seven times a day have I spoken your praise* (PSALM 119:164). [2] We will fulfill this sacred number of seven if at Lauds, Prime, Terce, Sext, None, Vespers and Compline we render the obligations of our office. [3] For it was of these hours of the day that he said, *Seven times a day have I spoken praise to you* (PSALM 119:164). [4] And concerning the nocturnal Vigil the same prophet said, *At midnight I arose to give thanks to you* (PSALM 119:62). [5] Therefore, at these times, we should offer praise to our creator for his just judgments: that is, at Lauds, Prime, Terce, Sext, None, Vespers and Compline; and *at night let us arise to give him praise* (PSALM 119:164,62).

CHAPTER 17: HOW MANY PSALMS ARE TO BE SUNG AT THESE HOURS

[1] We have already dealt with the order of psalmody for Vigils and Lauds. Let us now see to the remaining hours.

[2] At Prime three psalms are to be sung, separately and not with one 'Glory be.' [3] The hymn at this hour is to follow the opening versicle, *O God, come to my assistance* (PSALM 70:2), before the psalms are begun. [4] Then, after the three psalms are completed, one lesson is to be recited with a versicle, the 'Lord, have mercy,' and the dismissal.

[5] Tertia vero, sexta et nona, item eo ordine celebretur oratio, id est versu, hymnos earundem horarum, ternos psalmos, lectionem et versu, Kyrie eleison et missas. [6] Si maior congregatio fuerit, cum antiphonas, si vero minor, in directum psallantur.

[7] Vespertina autem synaxis quattuor psalmis cum antiphonis terminetur. [8] Post quibus psalmis, lectio recitanda est; inde responsorium, ambrosianum, versu, canticum de Evangelia, litania, et oratione dominica fiant missae.

[9] Completorios autem trium psalmorum dictione terminentur. Qui psalmi directanei sine antiphona dicendi sunt. [10] Post quos hymnum eiusdem horae, lectionem unam, versu, Kyrie eleison, et benedictione missae fiant.

XVIII QUO ORDINE IPSI PSALMI DICENDI SUNT

[1] In primis dicatur versu *Deus in adiutorium meum intende, Domine ad adiuvandum me festina*, gloria, inde hymnum uniuscuiusque horae. [2] Deinde, prima hora dominica, dicenda quattuor capitula psalmi centesimi octavi decimi; [3] reliquis vero horis, id est tertia, sexta vel nona, terna capitula suprascripti psalmi centesimi octavi decimi dicantur. [4] Ad primam autem secundae feriae, dicantur tres psalmi, id est primus, secundus et sextus; [5] et ita per singulos dies ad primam usque dominica dicantur per ordinem terni psalmi usque nonum decimum psalmum, ita sane ut nonus psalmus et septimus decimus partiantur in binos. [6] Et sic fit ut ad vigilias dominica semper a vicesimo incipiatur.

[5] **At Terce, Sext, and None prayer is celebrated the same way: that is, the verse, the hymn proper to each hour,** three psalms, **the lesson and versicle, the 'Lord, have mercy' and the dismissal.** [6] **If the community is rather large, the psalms are to be sung with refrains; if smaller, the psalms are sung straight through.**

[7] **The office of Vespers is limited to four psalms with refrains.** [8] **After these psalms a** lesson **is to be recited; then the** responsory, **the Ambrosian hymn and versicle, the canticle from the Gospel, the litany, and, the Lord's Prayer before the dismissal.**

[9] **Compline is limited to the recitation of** three psalms, **to be said straight through without refrains.** [10] **Then follows the hymn for that hour, one** lesson, the versicle, **the 'Lord, have mercy,' the blessing, and the dismissal.**

Feb 21; June 22; Oct 22

CHAPTER 18: IN WHAT ORDER THE PSALMS ARE TO BE SAID

[1] **At the beginning this verse is to be said:** *O God, come to my assistance; O Lord, make haste to help me* (PSALM 70:2) **with a 'Glory be,' followed by the hymn proper to each hour.** [2] **Then at Prime on Sunday four sections of Psalm One hundred and eighteen are said:** [3] **at the other hours, that is, Terce, Sext and None, three sections of this aforementioned Psalm One hundred and eighteen are said.** [4] **But at Prime on Monday three psalms are said: Psalms One, Two, and Six;** [5] **and so at Prime each day until Sunday three psalms are said in order, up to Psalm Twenty—Psalms Nine and Seventeen being each divided in two.** [6] **And so in this way Vigils on Sunday will always begin with Psalm Twenty.**

[7] Ad tertiam vero, sextam nonamque secundae feriae, novem capitula quae residua sunt de centesimo octavo decimo, ipsa terna per easdem horas dicantur. [8] Expenso ergo psalmo centesimo octavo decimo duobus diebus, id est dominico et secunda feria, [9] tertia feria iam ad tertiam, sextam vel nonam psallantur terni psalmi a centesimo nono decimo usque centesimo vicesimo septimo, id est psalmi novem. [10] Quique psalmi semper usque dominica per easdem horas itidem repetantur, hymnorum nihilominus, lectionum vel versuum dispositionem uniformem cunctis diebus servatam. [11] Et ita scilicet semper dominica a centesimo octavo decimo incipietur.

[12] Vespera autem cotidie quattuor psalmorum modulatione canatur. [13] Qui psalmi incipiantur a centesimo nono usque centesimo quadragesimo septimo, [14] exceptis his qui in diversis horis ex eis sequestrantur, id est a centesimo septimo decimo usque centesimo vicesimo septimo et centesimo tricesimo tertio et centesimo quadragesimo secundo; [15] reliqui omnes in vespera dicendi sunt. [16] Et quia minus veniunt tres psalmi, ideo dividendi sunt qui ex numero suprascripto fortiores inveniuntur, id est centesimum tricesimum octavum et centesimum quadragesimum tertium et centesimum quadragesimum quartum; [17] centesimus vero sextus decimus, quia parvus est, cum centesimo quinto decimo coniungatur.

Feb 22; June 23; Oct 23

[7] At Terce, Sext and None on Monday are said the nine remaining sections of Psalm One hundred and eighteen, three parts to be said at each hour. [8] Thus having completed Psalm One hundred and eighteen in two days (that is Sunday and Monday), [9] on Tuesday at Terce, Sext and None three psalms each are chanted from Psalm One hundred and nineteen through One hundred and twenty-seven, that is from nine psalms. [10] These psalms are always repeated until Sunday at the same hours every day: the disposition of hymns, lessons and versicles remains uniform on these days. [11] And so in this way Psalm One hundred and eighteen is always to begin on Sunday.

Feb 23; June 24; Oct 24

[12] Vespers is to be sung each day with four psalms, [13] These psalms are to begin with Psalm One hundred and nine and end at Psalm One hundred and forty–seven, [14] except for those already set apart for other hours: namely, Psalms One hundred and seventeen to One hundred and twenty–seven, Psalm One hundred and thirty–three and Psalm One hundred and forty–two; [15] all the rest are to be said at Vespers. [16] And as this leaves three psalms too few, those found to be of greater length as mentioned above should be divided: namely, Psalms One hundred and thirty–eight, One hundred and forty–three, and One hundred and forty–four. [17] Psalm One hundred and sixteen, which is short, should be joined to Psalm One hundred and fifteen.

[18] Digesto ergo ordine psalmorum vespertinorum, reliqua, id est lectionem, responsum, hymnum, versum vel canticum, sicut supra taxavimus impleatur. [19] Ad completorios vero cotidie idem psalmi repetantur, id est quartum, nonagesimum et centesimum tricesimum tertium.

[20] Disposito ordine psalmodiae diurnae, reliqui omnes psalmi qui supersunt aequaliter dividantur in septem noctium vigilias, [21] partiendo scilicet qui inter eos prolixiores sunt psalmi et duodecim per unamquamque constituens noctem.

[22] Hoc praecipue commonentes ut, si cui forte haec distributio psalmorum displicuerit, ordinet si melius aliter iudicaverit, [23] dum omnimodis id adtendat ut omni hebdomada psalterium ex integro numero centum quinquaginta psalmorum psallantur, et dominico die semper a caput reprehendatur ad vigilias. [24] Quia nimis inertem devotionis suae servitium ostendunt monachi qui minus a psalterio cum canticis consuetudinariis per septimanae circulum psallunt, [25] dum quando legamus sanctos patres nostros uno die hoc strenue implesse, quod nos tepidi utinam septimana integra persolvamus.

[18] Having thus arranged the order of psalms for Vespers, the rest—that is the lesson, responsory, hymn, versicle and canticle—is to be implemented as described above. [19] Each day at Compline the same psalms are repeated: that is Four, Ninety, and One hundred and thirty–three

Feb 24 (in Leap Year); June 24; Oct 24

[20] The order of psalmody at the day hours being thus disposed, all the remaining psalms are to be equally divided into seven nocturnal Vigils [21] by spitting the longer psalms in two and assigning twelve to each night.

[22] Above all we emphasize that if this distribution of the psalms is displeasing, one may order things differently as he judges better, [23] but by all means taking care that every week the psalter in its integral number of one hundred and fifty psalms is sung, and that on Sunday the cycle always begins anew at Vigils. [24] For those monks who show themselves sluggish in devotion to their service, singing less than the psalter with the customary canticles in the course of a week: [25] thus we read that our holy Fathers strenuously achieved in a single day what we, tepid as we are, take a whole week to render.

(RM 47:5-6, 8)

XIX DE DISCIPLINA PSALLENDI

[1] **Ubique credimus divinam esse praesentiam et** *oculos Domini in omni loco speculari bonos et malos,* [2] **maxime tamen hoc sine aliqua dubitatione credamus cum ad opus divinum assistimus.**

[3] **Ideo semper memores simus quod ait propheta:** *Servite Domino in* **timore,** [4] **et iterum:** *Psallite sapienter,* [5] **et:** *In conspectu angelorum psallam tibi.* [6] **Ergo consideremus qualiter oporteat in conspectu divinitatis et** angelorum **eius esse,** [7] **et sic stemus ad** psall**endum ut mens nostra concordet voci nostrae.**

(RM 48:1-2, 5, 10)

XX DE REVERENTIA ORATIONIS

[1] Si, **cum** hominibus **potentibus volumus aliqua suggerere, non praesumimus** nisi cum humilitate **et reverentia,** [2] quanto magis **Domino Deo universorum cum omni humilitate et puritatis devotione supplicandum est.** [3] Et non in multiloquio, **sed in puritate cordis et compunctione lacrimarum nos exaudiri sciamus.** [4] Et ideo brevis **debet esse et pura** oratio, **nisi forte ex affectu inspirationis divinae gratiae protendatur.** [5] In conventu tamen omnino brev**ietur** oratio, **et facto signo a priore omnes pariter surgant.**

Feb 24 (or 25); June 26; Oct 26

CHAPTER 19: THE DISCIPLINE OF CHANTING PSALMS

[1] We believe that the Divine Presence is everywhere, and *the eyes of the Lord in every place look upon the good and the evil* (PROVERBS 15:3). [2] We especially believe this without any doubt when we are assisting at the Work of God.

[3] Therefore let us always remember what the prophet says: *Serve the Lord in fear* (PSALM 2:11), and **again,** [4] *Chant psalms wisely* (PSALM 46:8); [5] and, *In the presence of the angels I will chant psalms to you* (PSALM 137:1). [6] Therefore let us consider how we ought to behave in the presence of the Holy One and His angels, [7] and thus stand to chant psalms in such a way that our mind and voice are in concord with each other.

Feb 25 (or 26); June 27; Oct 27

CHAPTER 20: REVERENCE IN PRAYER

[1] If when we wish to request something of powerful men we do not presume to do so except with humility and reverence, [2] how much more ought we to offer supplications to the universal Lord and God in all humility and purity of devotion? [3] And we know it is not on account of our wordiness that we are heard, but rather through purity of heart and tears of compunction. [4] And therefore prayer ought to be brief and pure, unless it happens to be prolonged by a sentiment inspired by divine grace. [5] In community, however, prayer should always be brief; and at the signal given by the superior all should rise together.

(RM 11:4, 14, 27)

XXI DE DECANIS MONASTERII

[1] Si maior fuerit congregatio, eligantur de ipsis fratres boni testimonii et sanctae conversationis, et constituantur decani, [2] qui sollicitudinem gerant super decanias suas in omnibus secundum mandata Dei et praecepta abbatis sui. [3] Qui decani tales eligantur in quibus securus abbas partiat onera sua, [4] et non eligantur per ordinem, sed secundum vitae meritum et sapientiae doctrinam.

[5] Quique decani, si ex eis aliqua forte quis inflatus superbia repertus fuerit reprehensibilis, correptus semel et iterum atque tertio si emendare noluerit, deiciatur, [6] et alter in loco eius qui dignus est surrogetur. [7] Et de praeposito eadem constituimus.

(RM 29:ti, 2-4; 11:109-114)

XXII QUOMODO DORMIANT MONACHI

[1] Singuli per singula lecta dormiant. [2] Lectisternia pro modo conversationis secundum dispensationem abbatis sui accipiant. [3] Si potest fieri omnes in uno loco dormiant; sin autem multitudo non sinit, deni aut viceni cum senioribus qui super eos solliciti sint pausent. [4] Candela iugiter in eadem cella ardeat usque mane.

CHAPTER 21: THE DEANS OF THE MONASTERY

[1] If the community is **large, there should be chosen from it brothers of good reputation and a holy way of life to be appointed deans:** [2] **They are to** carefully **oversee their deaneries in everything according to the commandments of God and the precepts of their abbot.** [3] **The ones chosen deans should be those with whom the abbot may confidently share his burdens:** [4] **thus they should not be chosen according to the order of seniority, but rather for the merit of their lives and their wise teaching.**

[5] **Should any of these deans become inflated with pride and be found to have acted reprehensibly; if, having been corrected once, twice, and even a third time, he refuses to amend, let him be deposed** [6] **and in his place there should be substituted another who is worthy.** [7] **And concerning the prior we establish that the same procedure is to be followed.**

CHAPTER 22: HOW THE MONKS ARE TO SLEEP

[1] **Each is to sleep in a separate bed.** [2] **They are to receive bedding appropriate to their way of life, according to the abbot's dispensation.** [3] **If possible, all should sleep in one place; but if their large numbers do not permit this they should sleep by tens or twenties with the seniors who are charged to watch over them.** [4] **A lamp should burn constantly in this room until morning.**

5 Vestiti dormiant et cincti cingellis **aut funibus, ut cultellos suos ad latus suum non habeant dum dormiunt**, ne **forte** per somnum **vulnerent dormientem;** 6 et ut parati sint **monachi semper et, facto signo absque mora** surgentes, **festinent** *invicem se praevenire* **ad opus Dei, cum omni tamen gravitate et modestia.** 7 **Adulescentiores fratres iuxta se non habeant lectos, sed permixti cum senioribus.** 8 **Surgentes vero ad opus Dei invicem se moderate cohortentur propter somnulentorum excusationes.**

(RM 12:1-3, 5)

XXIII DE EXCOMMUNICATIONE CULPARUM

1 Si quis frater contumax aut inoboediens aut superbus aut murmurans **vel in aliquo contrarius exsistens sanctae regulae et praeceptis seniorum suorum contemptor repertus fuerit,** 2 **hic** secundum **Domini nostri** praeceptum **admoneatur** semel et secundo **secrete a senioribus suis.** 3 Si non emendaverit, **obiurgetur publice coram omnibus.** 4 Si **vero neque sic correxerit, si intellegit qualis poena sit,** excommunicationi **subiaceat;** 5 sin autem **improbus est, vindictae corporali subdatur.**

[5] They are to sleep clothed and girded with belts **or cords, but they should** not **have their knives at their sides** while sleeping **lest they wound themselves in their sleep;** [6] **and thus monks will always be** prepared **when the signal is given to** rise **without delay, and to** *compete with one another* (ROMANS 12:10) **in hastening to the Work of God with all gravity and modesty.** [7] **The younger brethren should not have their beds next to each other, but interspersed among those of the seniors.** [8] **And upon arising for the Work of God they should quietly encourage one another, on account of the excuses which the sleepy tend to make.**

Feb 28 (or 29); June 30; Oct 30

CHAPTER 23: EXCOMMUNICATION FOR FAULTS

[1] If any brother is found to be contumacious, or disobedient, or proud, or a murmurer, **or in any way has contempt for the Holy Rule and the precepts of his seniors,** [2] **let him,** according to **Our Lord's** precept, **be admonished** once or twice **in private by his seniors** (*cf.* MATTHEW 18:15-16). [3] If he does not amend **he should be publicly rebuked in the presence of all.** [4] If **he still refuses to be corrected, he should (provided he understands what this penalty signifies) be subjected** to excommunication: [5] however, if **he lacks such understanding he should undergo corporal punishment.**

73

(RM 12:4-7; 13:50-67)

XXIV QUALIS DEBET ESSE MODUS EXCOMMUNICATIONIS

[1] Secundum **modum** culpae, **et** excommunicationis **vel disciplinae mensura debet extendi;** [2] **qui culparum modus in abbatis pendat iudicio.**

[3] **Si quis tamen** frater in levioribus culpis **invenitur,** a mensae **participatione privetur.** [4] **Privati autem a mensae consortio ista erit ratio ut in oratorio psalmum aut** antiphonam **non imponat, neque** lectionem **recitet, usque ad** satisfactionem. [5] **Refectionem autem cibi post fratrum refectionem solus accipiat,** [6] **ut, si verbi gratia fratres reficiunt sexta hora, ille frater nona, si fratres nona, ille vespera,** [7] **usque dum** satisfactione **congrua** veniam **consequatur.**

(RM 13:41-53)

XXV DE GRAVIORIBUS CULPIS

[1] **Is autem** frater qui gra**vioris** culpae **noxa tenetur suspendatur** a mensa, **simul ab oratorio.** [2] Nullus ei fratrum in nullo iungatur **consortio nec in colloquio.** [3] Solus sit **ad opus sibi iniunctum, persistens in paenitentiae luctu, sciens illam terribilem apostoli sententiam dicentis** [4] *traditum eiusmodi hominem in interitum carnis, ut spiritus salvus sit in die Domini.* [5] Cibi autem refectionem solus percipiat, **mensura vel hora qua praeviderit abbas ei competere;** [6] **nec a quoquam benedicatur** transeunte nec cibum quod ei datur.

CHAPTER 24: **ON THE DEGREES OF EXCOMMUNICATION**

[1] It is the degree of the fault which should serve as the measure of excommunication or discipline [2]—the degree of which fault is to be judged by the abbot.

[3] If any brother is found guilty of less serious faults he is to be deprived only of participation in the common table. [4] For one deprived of table-fellowship this shall be the norm: in the oratory he is to intone neither psalm nor refrain, nor may he recite a lesson until he has made satisfaction. [5] He is to receive his meals alone after the meal of the brothers. [6] Thus if, for example, the brothers eat at the sixth hour, this brother is to eat at the ninth hour; if they eat at the ninth hour, he is to eat at sundown, [7] until by proper satisfaction he obtains pardon.

CHAPTER 25: **MORE SERIOUS FAULTS**

[1] But that brother who is guilty of a more serious fault is to be suspended both from the common table and from the oratory. [2] None of the brothers may associate with him or engage him in conversation. [3] Laboring in solitude at the work enjoined on him, persisting in the sorrow of penitence, he is to consider that dreadful sentence of the apostle who says: [4] *such a man is handed over for the destruction of the flesh, so that the spirit may be saved on the day of the Lord* (I CORINTHIANS 5:5). [5] And his meals are to be taken alone, in the measure and at the hour the abbot considers best for him: [6] he may not be blessed by any who pass by, nor may the food be blessed that is given to him.

(RM 13:54-56)

XXVI DE HIS QUI SINE IUSSIONE IUNGUNT SE EXCOMMUNICATIS

[1] Si quis frater **praesumpserit sine iussione abbatis fratri excommunicato quolibet modo se iungere aut loqui cum eo vel mandatum ei dirigere,** [2] **similem** sortiatur excommunicationis **vindictam.**

(RM 14:7-8, 12; 15:26)

XXVII QUALITER DEBEAT ABBAS SOLLICITUS ESSE CIRCA EXCOMMUNICATOS

[1] **Omni sollicitudine curam gerat abbas circa delinquentes fratres, quia** *non est opus sanis medicus sed male habentibus.* [2] **Et ideo uti debet omni modo ut sapiens medicus, immittere senpectas, id est seniores sapientes fratres,** [3] **qui quasi secrete** consolentur fratrem fluctuantem et provocent ad humilitatis satisfactionem et *consolentur* **eum** *ne abundantiori tristitia absorbeatur,* [4] sed, sicut ait item apostolus, *confirmetur in eo caritas* et oretur pro eo ab omnibus.

[5] **Magnopere enim debet** sollicitudinem gerere **abbas et omni sagacitate et industria currere, ne aliquam de** ovibus sibi creditis **perdat.**

CHAPTER 26: THOSE WHO, WITHOUT PERMISSION, ASSOCIATE WITH THE EXCOMMUNICATED

[1] If a brother **presumes without permission from the abbot to associate in any way with an excommunicated brother, or to speak with him, or to send him a message,** [2] **he will incur the same kind of punishment** of excommunication.

CHAPTER 27: THE KIND OF SOLICITUDE THE ABBOT SHOULD HAVE FOR THE EXCOMMUNICATED

[1] **It is with all solicitude that the abbot should care for delinquent brothers, for** *it is not the healthy who have need of a physician, but those who are sick* (MATTHEW 9:12). [2] **And thus he should in every way act as a wise physician, sending** *senpectae,* **that is older and wise brothers,** [3] **who can, as it were in secret, console the wavering brother and convince him to make humble satisfaction, thus** *comforting* **him,** *lest he be devoured by excessive sorrow* (II CORINTHIANS 2:7); [4] **rather, as the apostle also says,** *Let love towards him be intensified* (II CORINTHIANS 2:8) **and let all pray for him.**

[5] **With the greatest possible** solicitude **the abbot should hasten to employ all wisdom and diligence so as not to lose any one of the** sheep entrusted **to him.**

[6] Noverit enim se infirmarum curam suscepisse animarum, non super sanas tyrannidem; [7] et metuat prophetae comminationem per quam dicit Deus: *Quod crassum videbatis assumebatis et quod debile erat proiciebatis.* [8] Et pastoris boni pium imitetur exemplum, qui, relictis nonaginta novem ovibus in montibus, abiit unam ovem quae erraverat quaerere; [9] cuius infirmitati in tantum compassus est, ut eam *in sacris humeris suis* dignaretur *imponere* et sic reportare ad gregem.

(RM 13:68-73)

XXVIII DE HIS QUI SAEPIUS CORREPTI EMENDARE NOLUERINT

[1] Si quis frater frequenter correptus pro qualibet culpa, si etiam excommunicatus non emendaverit, acrior ei accedat correptio, id est ut verberum vindicta in eum procedant. [2] Quod si nec ita correxerit, aut forte— quod absit—in superbia elatus etiam defendere voluerit opera sua, tunc abbas faciat quod sapiens medicus: [3] si exhibuit fomenta, si unguenta adhortationum, si medicamina scripturarum divinarum, si ad ultimum ustionem excommunicationis vel plagarum virgae, [4] et iam si viderit nihil suam praevalere industriam, adhibeat etiam—quod maius est— suam et omnium fratrum pro eo orationem, [5] ut Dominus qui omnia potest operetur salutem circa infirmum fratrem.

[6] For he should know that he has undertaken to care for weak souls, not to exercise tyranny over the strong; [7] and he ought to fear the threat of the prophet in which God says: *What you saw to be fat you took for youselves, and what was injured you cast away* (EZEKIEL 34:10,4-6). [8] And he should imitate the loving example of the good shepherd, who, leaving the ninety–nine sheep on the mountains, went to seek the one which had lost its way: [9] its weakness inspired such compassion that *He* deigned *to place it on His* own sacred *shoulders* and thus carry it back to the flock (LUKE 15:5).

Mar 5; July 5; Nov 4

CHAPTER 28: THOSE WHO, DESPITE FREQUENT CORRECTION, DO NOT AMEND

[1] If a brother who is frequently corrected for some fault, or even excommunicated, does not amend, he should receive a more severe correction: that is, let the punishment of beatings be administered to him. [2] If he then does not correct himself, or even (may it not happen!) inflamed with pride, he wishes to defend his actions, then the abbot should act as a wise physician: [3] if he has applied compresses and the ointment of his admonitions, the medicine of the Sacred Scriptures, and ultimately the cautery of excommunication or strokes of the rod; [4] and if he still sees that his labors are unavailing, he should add what is even greater—his prayers and those of all the brethren for him, [5] that the Lord who is can do all things may effect the healing of the sick brother.

[6] Quod si nec isto modo sanatus fuerit, tunc iam utatur abbas ferro abscisionis, ut ait apostolus: *Auferte malum ex vobis,* [7] et iterum: *Infidelis, si discedit, discedat,* [8] ne una ovis morbida omnem gregem contagiet.

(RM 64:1-4)

XXIX   SI DEBEANT FRATRES EXEUNTES DE MONASTERIO ITERUM RECIPI

[1] Frater qui proprio vitio egreditur de monasterio, si reverti voluerit, spondeat prius omnem emendationem pro quo egressus est, [2] et sic in ultimo gradu recipiatur, ut ex hoc eius humilitas comprobetur. [3] Quod si denuo exierit, usque tertio ita recipiatur, iam postea sciens omnem sibi reversionis aditum denegari.

(RM 14:79-86)

XXX   DE PUERIS MINORI AETATE, QUALITER CORRIPIANTUR

[1] Omnis aetas vel intellectus proprias debet habere mensuras. [2] Ideoque, quotiens pueri vel adulescentiores aetate, aut qui minus intellegere possunt quanta poena sit excommunicationis, [3] hi tales dum delinquunt, aut ieiuniis nimiis affligantur aut acris verberibus coerceantur, ut sanentur.

[6] But if even by this means he is not healed, then the abbot may use the knife for amputation, as the apostle says: *Banish the evil one from you* (I CORINTHIANS 5:13), and again: [7] *If the unfaithful one departs, let him depart* (I CORINTHIANS 7:15), [8] lest one diseased sheep infect the whole flock.

Mar 6; July 6; Nov 5

CHAPTER 29: WHETHER BROTHERS WHO LEAVE THE MONASTERY MAY BE READMITTED

[1] If a brother who through his own evil action departs from the monastery, then wishes to return, he should first promise the complete amendment of that which caused his departure. [2] Then he is to be received back in the lowest place, so that in this way his humility may be tried. [3] If he should again depart, he may be received back up to the third time; but after this he must know that all possibility of return will be denied him.

Mar 7; July 7; Nov 6

CHAPTER 30: HOW CHILDREN OF TENDER YEARS ARE TO BE CORRECTED

[1] Every age and intellectual capacity should receive the measure proper to it. [2] Thus with regard to boys or adolescents or those who lack the ability to understand the significance of the penalty of excommunication, [3] when these commit faults they are to be afflicted with severe fasting or chastised with sharp strokes so they may be healed.

(RM 16:27-37, 62-66)

XXXI DE CELLARARIO MONASTERII, QUALIS SIT

[1] Cellararius **monasterii eligatur de congregatione, sapiens, maturis moribus, sobrius,** non multum **edax, non elatus, non turbulentus, non iniuriosus, non tardus, non prodigus,** [2] sed timens Deum; qui omni congregationi sit sicut pater. [3] Curam gerat de omnibus; [4] sine iussione abbatis nihil faciat. [5] Quae iubentur custodiat; [6] fratres non contristet. [7] Si quis frater ab eo forte aliqua irrationabiliter postulat, non spernendo eum contristet, sed rationabiliter cum humilitate male petenti deneget. [8] Animam suam custodiat, memor semper illud apostolicum quia *qui bene ministraverit gradum bonum sibi acquirit.*

[9] **Infirmorum, infantum, hospitum pauperumque cum omni sollicitudine curam gerat, sciens sine dubio quia pro his omnibus in die iudicii rationem redditurus est.** [10] **Omnia** vasa monasterii cunctamque substantiam ac si altaris vasa sacrata **conspiciat.** [11] **Nihil ducat neglegendum.** [12] **Neque avaritiae studeat, neque prodigus sit et stirpator substantiae monasterii, sed omnia mensurate faciat et secundum iussionem abbatis.**

CHAPTER 31: THE QUALITIES OF THE MONASTERY CELLARER

[1] As monastery cellarer there should be chosen from the community one who is wise, of mature character, temperate, not an excessive eater, not haughty, not turbulent, not harmful, not sluggish, not wasteful, [2] but God–fearing; one who can act as a father to the whole community. [3] He is to have charge of everything; [4] he is to do nothing without an order from the abbot. [5] He is to keep custody over his orders; [6] he is not to sadden the brothers. [7] If one of the brothers happens to request something unreasonably, he is not to treat him with disdain and thus sadden him, rather he must reasonably and with humility deny the bad request. [8] He is to keep custody over his own soul, remembering always that apostolic saying: *he who has ministered well acquires a good standing for himself* (I TIMOTHY 3:13).

[9] He is to care for the sick, for children, for guests, and for the poor with all solicitude, knowing without doubt that for all these *he will have to give an account* on the Day of Judgment (*cf.* LUKE 16:2) [10] He is to look upon all the vessels and goods of the monastery as though they were the sacred vessels of the altar. [11] He is not to neglect anything. [12] He is not to be avaricious, not wasteful, not be a squanderer of the monastery's resources; rather he is to do everything in proper measure and according to the order of his abbot.

(RM 16:19, 27-37)

[13] Humilitatem ante omnia habeat, et cui substantia non est quod tribuatur, sermo responsionis porrigatur bonus, [14] ut scriptum est: *Sermo bonus super datum optimum.*

[15] Omnia quae ei iniunxerit abbas, ipsa habeat sub cura sua; a quibus eum prohibuerit, non praesumat. [16] Fratribus constitutam annonam sine aliquo typho vel mora offerat, ut non scandalizentur, memor divini eloquii quid mereatur *qui scandalizaverit unum de pusillis.*

[17] Si congregatio maior fuerit, solacia ei dentur, a quibus adiutus et ipse aequo animo impleat officium sibi commissum. [18] Horis competentibus dentur quae danda sunt et petantur quae petenda sunt, [19] ut nemo perturbetur neque contristetur in domo Dei.

Mar 9; July 9; Nov 8

13 **Above all else he is to have humility: when he has nothing material to give to one who makes a request he is to offer at least a kind word,** 14 **as it is written:** *A* kind *word is higher than the best gift* (SIRACH 18:17).

15 **All that the abbot has entrusted to him he is to have in his care, and he is not to presume to do what has been forbidden him.** 16 **To the brethren he is to offer their** allotted ration **of food without condescension or delay, so that they are not scandalized, remembering what the Sacred Text says is merited by one who** *scandalizes one of these little ones* (MATTHEW 18:6).

17 **If the community is large, helpers are to be given to him, thanks to whose assistance he may retain a peaceful soul while fulfilling the office committed to him.** 18 **Only at the appropriate hours are items for distribution to be distributed, or requested items to be requested;** 19 **so that no one is perturbed or saddened in the house of God.**

XXXII DE FERRAMENTIS VEL REBUS MONASTERII

[1] **Substantia** monasterii **in ferramentis vel vestibus seu quibuslibet rebus praevideat abbas fratres de quorum vita et moribus securus sit,** [2] **et eis singula, ut utile iudicaverit, consignet custodienda atque recolligenda.** [3] **Ex quibus** abbas brevem teneat, ut **dum sibi in ipsa assignata fratres vicissim succedunt, sciat quid dat aut quid recipit.**

[4] **Si quis autem sordide aut neglegenter res monasterii tractaverit, corripiatur;** [5] **si non emendaverit, disciplinae regulari subiaceat.**

(RM 16:58; 82:16-27)

XXXIII SI QUID DEBEANT **MONACHI PROPRIUM** HABERE

[1] **Praecipue hoc vitium radicitus amputandum est de monasterio,** [2] **ne quis praesumat aliquid dare aut accipere sine iussione abbatis,** [3] **neque aliquid habere proprium, nullam omnino rem, neque codicem, neque tabulas, neque graphium, sed nihil omnino,** [4] **quippe quibus nec corpora sua nec voluntates licet habere in propria voluntate;** [5] **omnia vero** necessaria **a patre sperare monasterii, nec quicquam liceat habere quod abbas non dederit aut permiserit.** [6] *Omniaque* omnium *sint communia,* ut scriptum est, *ne quisquam suum aliquid dicat* vel praesumat.

CHAPTER 32: THE TOOLS AND POSSESSIONS OF THE MONASTERY

1 The abbot is to provide for the material goods of the monastery—that is tools, clothes, and any other thing—by means of brothers whose life and character he trusts; 2 and he is to consign to them the different items as he judges best, to be conserved and then collected after use. 3 Of these items the abbot is to keep a list, so that as the brothers are successively assigned to different tasks, he will know what he gives out and what he receives back.

4 If anyone treats the goods of the monastery improperly or negligently he is to be corrected; 5 if he does not amend, he is to be subjected to the discipline of the Rule.

CHAPTER 33: WHETHER MONKS SHOULD HAVE ANYTHING OF THEIR OWN

1 Above all this vice is to be cut out by the roots from the monastery, 2 no one may presume to give or receive anything without the abbot's order 3 nor to have anything as their own—not anything— neither book, writing–tablet, pen, nor anything at all 4 since it is not allowed that even their body or their will should remain subject to their own will: 5 rather, for all necessary things let them trust to the father of the monastery, since none of them is allowed to have anything which the abbot has not given or permitted. 6 *All things are to be held in common* by all, as it is written, *so that no one may say* or presume *that anything is his own* (ACTS 4:32).

[7] Quod si quisquam huic nequissimo vitio deprehensus fuerit delectari, admoneatur semel et iterum; [8] si non emendaverit, correptioni subiaceat.

XXXIV SI OMNES AEQUALITER DEBEANT NECESSARIA ACCIPERE

[1] Sicut scriptum est: Dividebatur singulis prout cuique opus erat. [2] Ubi non dicimus ut personarum quod absit acceptio sit, sed infirmitatum consideratio; [3] ubi qui minus indiget agat Deo gratias et non contristetur, [4] qui vero plus indiget humilietur pro infirmitate, non extollatur pro misericordia; [5] et ita omnia membra erunt in pace. [6] Ante omnia, ne murmurationis malum pro qualicumque causa in aliquo qualicumque verbo vel significatione appareat; [7] quod si deprehensus fuerit, districtiori disciplinae subdatur.

(RM 18:1-12; 19:19-27; 16:39-40)

XXXV DE SEPTIMANARIIS COQUINAE

[1] Fratres sibi invicem serviant, ut nullus excusetur a coquinae officio, nisi aut aegritudo, aut in causa gravis utilitatis quis occupatus fuerit, [2] quia exinde maior merces et caritas acquiritur. [3] Imbecillibus autem procurentur solacia, ut non cum tristitia hoc faciant; [4] sed habeant omnes solacia secundum modum congregationis aut positionem loci.

[7] But if anyone is found engaging in this most destructive vice he is to be admonished once or twice: [8] if he does not amend he is to be subjected to correction.

CHAPTER 34: WHETHER ALL SHOULD RECEIVE NECESSARY THINGS EQUALLY

[1] As it is written: *Distribution was made to each one according to his need.* (Acts 4:35). [2] We do not mean by this that there should be personal favoritism (may it never happen!) but rather that infirmities should be taken into consideration: [3] thus one who requires less should give thanks to God and be not saddend; [4] and one who requires more should be humbled because of his infirmity—not exalted by the mercy shown him, [5] and in this way all the members may be at peace. [6] Above all, the evil of murmuring must not appear for any reason, through any word or sign whatever: [7] someone found guilty of this is to be subjected to very severe discipline.

CHAPTER 35: THE WEEKLY KITCHEN SERVERS

[1] The brothers are to serve one another; thus no one is to be excused from kitchen duties unless he is ill, except in the case of one occupied with some matter of great importance: [2] for in this way great reward and love are acquired. [3] For the feeble, however, assistance is to be procured so they do not become discouraged; [4] indeed, all are to have assistance according to the size of the community and local conditions.

[5] Si maior congregatio fuerit, **cellararius excusetur a coquina, vel si qui, ut diximus, maioribus utilitatibus occupantur;** [6] **ceteri sibi sub caritate invicem serviant.**

[7] **Egressurus de septimana sabbato munditias faciat.** [8] **Lintea cum quibus sibi fratres manus aut pedes tergunt lavent.** [9] **Pedes vero tam ipse qui egreditur quam ille qui intraturus est omnibus lavent.** [10] **Vasa ministerii sui munda et sana cellarario reconsignet;** [11] **qui cellararius item intranti consignet, ut sciat quod dat aut quod** recipit.

(RM 25:3-7; 19:1-8)

[12] **Septimanarii autem ante unam horam refectionis accipiant super statutam annonam singulas biberes et panem,** [13] **ut hora refectionis sine murmuratione et gravi labore serviant fratribus suis.** [14] **In diebus tamen sollemnibus usque ad missas sustineant.**

[15] **Intrantes et exeuntes hebdomadarii in oratorio mox matutinis finitis dominica omnibus genibus provolvantur postulantes pro se orari.** [16] **Egrediens autem de septimana dicat hunc versum:** *Benedictus es, Domine Deus, qui adiuvasti me et consolatus es me;* [17] **quo dicto tertio accepta benedictione egrediens, subsequatur ingrediens et dicat:** *Deus in adiutorium meum intende, Domine ad adiuvandum me festina,* [18] **et hoc idem tertio repetatur ab omnibus et accepta benedictione ingrediatur.**

⁵ If the community is large, **the cellarer is to be excused from kitchen service, together with any others who are occupied (as we have said) with matters of greater importance:** ⁶ the rest are to serve one another in love.

⁷ The one completing his week is to do the cleaning on Saturday. ⁸ They are to wash the towels with which the brothers wipe their hands and feet. ⁹ Both the one who is finishing his service and the one about to begin are to wash the feet of all. ¹⁰ He is to return to the cellerar, clean and in good condition, the vessels used in his work; the cellarer is then to consign them to the one beginning his service, ¹¹ so that he knows what he gives out and what he receives back.

Mar 14; July 14; Nov 13

¹² An hour before the meal the weekly servers are to receive, over and above the usual allowance, a drink and a piece of bread, ¹³ so that at meal time they may serve the brothers without murmuring or oppressive exertion. ¹⁴ On solemn days, however, they are to wait until after the dismissal.

¹⁵ On Sunday as soon as Lauds has ended, both those beginning and those completing their week shall bow before the knees of all, asking for their prayers. ¹⁶ The one ending his week is to say this verse: *Blessed are you, Lord God, who have helped me and consoled me* (DANIEL 3:52; PSALM 86:17); ¹⁷ and having said this three times, the one ending his service is to receive the blessing. The one beginning his service then continues, saying: *O God, come to my assistance; O Lord, make haste to help me* (PSALM 70:2), ¹⁸ and when this has been repeated three times by all, and having then received the blessing, he is to begin his service.

(RM 70:3)

XXXVI DE INFIRMIS FRATRIBUS

[1] Infirmorum cura ante omnia et super omnia adhibenda est, ut sicut revera Christo ita eis serviatur, [2] quia ipse dixit: *Infirmus fui et visitastis me,* [3] et: *Quod fecistis uni de his minimis mihi fecistis.* [4] Sed et ipsi infirmi considerent in honorem Dei sibi servire, et non superfluitate sua contristent fratres suos servientes sibi; [5] qui tamen patienter portandi sunt, quia de talibus copiosior merces acquiritur. [6] Ergo cura maxima sit abbati ne aliquam neglegentiam patiantur.

[7] Quibus fratribus infirmis sit cella super se deputata et servitor timens Deum et diligens ac sollicitus. [8] Balnearum usus infirmis quotiens expedit offeratur—sanis autem et maxime iuvenibus tardius concedatur. [9] Sed et carnium esus infirmis omnino debilibus pro reparatione concedatur; at, ubi meliorati fuerunt, a carnibus more solito omnes abstineant.

[10] Curam autem maximam habeat abbas ne a cellarariis aut a servitoribus neglegantur infirmi. Et ipsum respicit quicquid a discipulis delinquitur.

Mar 15; July 15; Nov 14

CHAPTER 36: THE SICK BROTHERS

[1] Care of the sick must rank before and above everything, so that they may truly be served as Christ Himself, [2] for He said: *I was sick and you visited me* (MATTHEW 25:36) [3] and, *Whatever you did for one of these who are least, you did for me* (MATTHEW 25:40). [4] But let the sick themselves consider that they are served out of honor for God, and they are not to sadden their brothers who serve them with superfluous demands; [5] Yet they are to be patiently borne, because from such as these a more abundant reward is acquired. [6] The abbot shall therefore exercise the greatest care that they not suffer any neglect.

[7] These brothers who are sick are to be assigned a separate room and a God-fearing attendant who is also diligent and solicitous. [8] Baths may be offered the sick whenever this is helpful, but those who are healthy, especially the young are to be allowed this less frequently. [9] Additionally, the sick who are very weak may be allowed to eat meat to recover their strength; but when they are better, all are to abstain from meat as usual.

[10] Moreover the abbot is to maintain the greatest care that that the sick are not neglected by the cellarers or attendants. For he is responsible for whatever is lacking in his disciples.

(RM 28:19-26)

XXXVII DE SENIBUS VEL INFANTIBUS

[1] Licet ipsa natura humana trahatur ad misericordiam in his aetatibus, senum videlicet et infantum, tamen et regulae auctoritas eis prospiciat. [2] Consideretur semper in eis imbecillitas et ullatenus eis districtio regulae teneatur in alimentis, [3] sed sit in eis pia consideratio et praeveniant horas canonicas.

(RM 24:14, 30, 40)

XXXVIII DE HEBDOMADARIO LECTORE

[1] Mensis fratrum lectio deesse non debet, nec fortuito casu qui arripuerit codicem legere ibi, sed lecturus tota hebdomada dominica ingrediatur. [2] Qui ingrediens post missas et communionem petat ab omnibus pro se orari, ut avertat ab ipso Deus spiritum elationis, [3] et dicatur hic versus in oratorio tertio ab omnibus, ipso tamen incipiente: *Domine, labia mea aperies, et os meum adnuntiabit laudem tuam;* [4] et sic accepta benedictione ingrediatur ad legendum.

[5] Et summum fiat silentium, ut nullius mussitatio vel vox nisi solius legentis ibi audiatur. [6] Quae vero necessaria sunt comedentibus et bibentibus sic sibi vicissim ministrent fratres ut nullus indigeat petere aliquid; [7] si quid tamen opus fuerit, sonitu cuiuscumque signi potius petatur quam voce.

CHAPTER 37: **THE AGED AND CHILDREN**

[1] Although human nature is of itself drawn towards compassion for these two ages—the aged and children—the authority of the Rule should also provide for them. [2] Their weakness should always be considered, and they are in no way required to adhere to the full rigor of the Rule concerning diet: [3] rather, caring consideration is to be shown them, and they are to anticipate the regular hours.

CHAPTER 38: THE WEEKLY READER

[1] At the brothers' table there should always be reading, but this is not to be done carelessly by one who simply grabs for the book and reads; rather let the reader is to begin a whole week's service on Sunday. [2] The one who begins his service is to ask after Mass and Communion that all pray for him, that God may protect him from the spirit of pride: [3] and this verse is to be said three times in the oratory by all after the reader begins it: *O Lord, open my lips, and my mouth shall declare your praise* (PSALM 51:17); [4] and thus receiving the blessing he begins his service of reading.

[5] And total silence is to be kept, so that no whispering or voice may be heard there except that of the reader alone. [6] With regard to things necessary for eating and drinking the brothers are to minister to one another in turn, so that no one need ask for anything: [7] If anything is wanted, it should be asked for by some audible sign rather than in words.

⁸ Nec praesumat ibi aliquis de ipsa lectione aut aliunde quicquam requirere, *ne detur occasio;* ⁹ nisi forte prior pro aedificatione voluerit aliquid breviter dicere.

¹⁰ Frater autem lector hebdomadarius accipiat mixtum priusquam incipiat legere, propter communionem sanctam, et ne forte grave sit ei ieiunium sustinere. ¹¹ Postea autem cum coquinae hebdomadariis et servitoribus reficiat.

¹² Fratres autem non per ordinem legant aut cantent, sed qui aedificant audientes.

(RM 26:3, 11-14)

XXXIX DE MENSURA CIBUS

¹ Sufficere credimus ad refectionem cotidianam tam sextae quam nonae, omnibus mensis, cocta duo pulmentaria, propter diversorum infirmitatibus, ² ut forte qui ex illo non potuerit edere ex alio reficiatur. ³ Ergo duo pulmentaria cocta fratribus omnibus sufficiant et, si fuerit unde poma aut nascentia leguminum, addatur et tertium. ⁴ Panis libra una propensa sufficiat in die, sive una sit refectio sive prandii et cenae: ⁵ quod si cenaturi sunt, de eadem libra tertia pars a cellarario servetur reddenda cenandis.

⁶ Quod si labor forte factus fuerit maior, in arbitrio et potestate abbatis erit, si expediat, aliquid augere, ⁷ remota prae omnibus crapula et ut numquam surripiat monacho indigeries, ⁸ quia nihil sic contrarium est omni christiano quomodo crapula,

[8] No one is to presume there to ask any question about the reading or anything else, *lest occasion be given* (EPHESIANS 4:27; I TIMOTHY 5:4); [9] unless perhaps the superior wishes to briefly say something edifying.

[10] However, the brother who is reader for the week is to receive mixed wine and water before he begins to read, on account of Holy Communion and so that it is not oppressive for him to continue his fast. [11] Afterwards he is to dine with the weekly kitchen servers and attendants.

[12] The brothers, however, are not to read or sing according to their rank, but only those who edify the hearers.

Mar 18; July 18; Nov 17

CHAPTER 39: THE MEASURE OF FOOD

[1] We believe it will suffice for the daily meal, whether at the sixth or ninth hour, that there be on all tables two dishes of cooked food on account of the variety of illnesses: [2] so that he who is not be able to eat one may make his meal of the other. [3] Therefore two cooked dishes will suffice for all the brothers; and if there is any fruit or young vegetables, a third dish is be added. [4] A liberal pound of bread should suffice each day, whether there is only one meal or both lunch and dinner: [5] and if they are to have dinner, a third part of their pound is to be kept back by the cellarer, and returned to them at dinner.

[6] If it happens that the work is heavier the abbot can choose to exercise his power, when expedient, to add something, [7] provided that before all else overindulgence is avoided, and that no monk suffers indigestion. [8] For nothing is more contrary to all things Christian than overindulgence,

[9] sicut ait Dominus noster: *Videte ne graventur corda vestra crapula.*

[10] Pueris vero minori aetate non eadem servetur quantitas, sed minor quam maioribus, servata in omnibus parcitate.

[11] Carnium vero quadrupedum omnimodo ab omnibus abstineatur comestio, praeter omnino debiles aegrotos.

(RM 27:39, 43-47)

XL DE MENSURA POTUS

[1] Unusquisque proprium habet donum ex Deo, alius sic, alius vero sic; [2] et ideo cum aliqua scrupulositate a nobis mensura victus aliorum constituitur. [3] Tamen infirmorum contuentes imbecillitatem, credimus heminam vini per singulos sufficere per diem. [4] Quibus autem donat Deus tolerantiam abstinentiae, propriam se habituros mercedem sciant.

[5] Quod si aut loci necessitas vel labor aut ardor aestatis amplius poposcerit, in arbitrio prioris consistat, considerans in omnibus ne surrepat satietas aut ebrietas. [6] Licet legamus vinum omnino monachorum non esse, sed quia nostris temporibus id monachis persuaderi non potest, saltem vel hoc consentiamus ut non usque ad satietatem bibamus, sed parcius, [7] quia vinum apostatare facit etiam sapientes.

[8] Ubi autem necessitas loci exposcit ut nec suprascripta mensura inveniri possit, sed multo minus aut ex toto nihil, benedicant Deum qui ibi habitant et non murmurent. [9] Hoc ante omnia admonentes ut absque murmurationibus sint.

[9] as Our Lord says: *See that your hearts are not weighed down through overindulgence* (LUKE 21:34).

[10] To children of immature years the same quantity should not be given: instead, they should receive less than their elders, frugality being observed in all matters.

[11] But all are to abstain from eating the flesh of four—footed animals, **except the sick who are very weak.**

Mar 19; July 19; Nov 18

CHAPTER 40: THE MEASURE OF DRINK

[1] Everyone has *his proper gift from God: one this, another that* (I CORINTHIANS 7:7); [2] and it is therefore with some reluctance that we fix the measure for another. [3] However, taking into account the weakness of some, we believe that a hemina of wine for each will suffice each day. [4] But those to whom God gives the strength to abstain should know that they will earn their proper reward.

[5] If local necessity, or the work, or the heat of summer suggest that more is advisable, the matter rests with the will of the superior, care being taken in everything that satiety or drunkenness not sneak in. [6] Even though we read that wine is certainly not for monks, yet, since in our days monks cannot be persuaded of this we must at least agree not to drink to satiety, but frugally, [7] for wine makes even the wise fall away (SIRACH 19:2).

[8] But where local necessities are such that even the above-mentioned measure cannot be supplied, and instead there is much less or nothing at all, those who dwell there are to bless God and not murmur. [9] This we admonish above everything else: that they refrain from murmuring.

(RM 28:1-2, 8, 37)

XLI QUIBUS HORIS OPORTET REFICERE FRATRES

[1] A sancto Pascha usque Pentecosten, ad sextam reficiant fratres et sera cenent. [2] A Pentecosten autem, tota aestate, si labores agrorum non habent monachi aut nimietas aestatis non perturbat, quarta et sexta feria ieiunent usque ad nonam; [3] reliquis diebus ad sextam prandeant; [4] quam prandii sextam, si operis in agris habuerint aut aestatis fervor nimius fuerit, continuanda erit et in abbatis sit providentia. [5] Et sic omnia temperet atque disponat qualiter et animae salventur et quod faciunt fratres absque iusta murmuratione faciant.

[6] Ab idus autem Septembres usque caput quadragesimae, ad nonam semper reficiant. [7] In quadragesima vero usque in Pascha, ad vesperam reficiant; [8] ipsa tamen vespera sic agatur ut lumen lucernae non indigeant reficientes, sed luce adhuc diei omnia consummentur. [9] Sed et omni tempore, sive cena sive refectionis hora sic temperetur ut luce fiant omnia.

Mar 20; July 20; Nov 19

CHAPTER 41: AT WHAT HOURS THE BROTHERS ARE TO TAKE THEIR MEALS

[1] From holy Easter until Pentecost the brothers are to take their meal at the sixth hour and in the evening eat supper. [2] However, from Pentecost throughout the summer if the monks do not have field labor and are not troubled by excessive heat, they are to fast on Wednesdays and Fridays until the ninth hour, [3] and on other days eat lunch at the sixth hour: [4] lunch at the sixth hour is to be maintained if they have work in the fields or if the summer heat is excessive, and it up to the abbot to provide for this. [5] And he is similarly to adjust and dispose everything so that souls may be saved and the brothers may perform their activities without any justifiable murmuring.

[6] From September thirteenth until the beginning of Lent the meal is always to be at the ninth hour. [7] From Lent until Easter, however, they are to have their meal just before Vespers: [8] but Vespers is thus to be celebrated in such a way that they do not need lamp-light while eating; instead everything is to be completed by daylight. [9] Indeed, in all seasons the hour for dinner or for the meal is to be adjusted so that everything can be done while there is still light.

(RM 30:11, 17, 19-20)

XLII UT POST COMPLETORIUM NEMO LOQUATUR

[1] Omni tempore silentium debent studere monachi, maxime tamen nocturnis horis. [2] Et ideo omni tempore, sive ieiunii sive prandii: [3] si tempus fuerit prandii, mox surrexerint a cena, sedeant omnes in unum et legat unus Collationes vel Vitas Patrum aut certe aliud quod aedificet audientes, [4] non autem Heptateuchum aut Regum, quia infirmis intellectibus non erit utile illa hora hanc scripturam audire, aliis vero horis legantur.

[5] Si autem ieiunii dies fuerit, dicta vespera parvo intervallo mox accedant ad lectionem Collationum, ut diximus. [6] Et lectis quattuor aut quinque foliis vel quantum hora permittit, [7] omnibus in unum occurrentibus per hanc moram lectionis, si qui forte in assignato sibi commisso fuit occupatus, [8] omnes ergo in unum positi compleant et, exeuntes a completoriis, nulla sit licentia denuo cuiquam loqui aliquid— [9] quod si inventus fuerit quisquam praevaricare hanc taciturnitatis regulam, gravi vindictae subiaceat—[10] excepto si necessitas hospitum supervenerit aut forte abbas alicui aliquid iusserit, [11] quod tamen et ipsud cum summa gravitate et moderatione honestissima fiat.

Mar 21; July 21; Nov 20

CHAPTER 42: NO ONE IS TO SPEAK AFTER COMPLINE

[1] At all times silence is to be studiously kept by monks, especially during the hours of night. [2] And this is to be the case in all seasons, whether fast days or days with a noon meal: [3] if it is a day with a noon meal, as soon as they have risen from dinner all are to be seated together and someone is to read from the *Conferences* or *Lives of the Fathers*, or something else which will edify the hearers; [4] but not from the Heptateuch or Kings, since it is not helpful for those of weak understanding to hear those parts of Scripture at that hour: they should be read at other hours.

[5] If it is a fast-day, then after a brief interval following the saying of Vespers they are to gather for the reading of the *Conferences* as we have said. [6] And having read five or four pages, as the hour permits, [7] all are to gather during the interval provided by this reading, even those occupied in some assigned project: [8] when all have gathered together they are to say Compline; and when they go out from Compline no one is allowed to say anything further to anyone; [9] but if anyone is found evading this rule concerning restraint of speech he is to be severely punished, [10] unless the necessities of guests supervened or the abbot gave someone a command: [11] but even this is to be done with the greatest seriousness and proper moderation.

(RM 54:1-2,; 73:2-6)

XLIII DE HIS QUI AD OPUS DEI VEL AD MENSAM TARDE OCCURRUNT

[1] **Ad** horam divini officii, mox **auditus fuerit signus, relictis omnibus quaelibet fuerint in manibus, summa cum festinatione curratur,** [2] **cum gravitate tamen, ut non scurrilitas inveniat fomitem.** [3] **Ergo** *nihil* **operi Dei** *praeponatur.*

[4] **Quod si quis in nocturnis vigiliis post gloriam psalmi nonagesimi quarti, quem propter hoc omnino subtrahendo et morose volumus dici, occurrerit, non stet in ordine suo in choro,** [5] **sed ultimus omnium stet aut in loco quem talibus neglegentibus seorsum constituerit abbas, ut videantur ab ipso vel ab omnibus,** [6] **usque dum completo opere Dei publica** satisfactione **paeniteat.**

[7] Ideo autem eos in ultimo aut seorsum iudicavimus **debere stare ut, visi ab omnibus, vel pro ipsa** verecundia sua emendent; [8] nam, si foris oratorium **remaneant, erit forte talis qui se aut recollocet et dormit, aut certe sedit sibi foris vel fabulis vacat, et datur occasio maligno;** [9] **sed ingrediantur intus, ut nec totum perdant et** de **reliquo** emendent.

[10] **Diurnis autem horis, qui ad opus Dei post versum et gloriam primi psalmi qui post versum dicitur non occurrerit, lege qua supra diximus in ultimo stent,** [11] **nec praesumant sociari choro psallentium usque ad satisfactionem, nisi forte abbas licentiam dederit remissione sua,** [12] **ita tamen ut satisfaciat reus ex hoc.**

CHAPTER 43: **THOSE** WHO ARRIVE LATE AT THE WORK OF GOD **OR AT TABLE**

[1] At the hour **for the** Divine Office as soon as the **signal** is heard, he is to lay aside everything he is doing with his hands and hasten with all speed, [2] and yet seriously, so that no occasion is provided for ridiculing. [3] Thus *nothing is to be preferred* to the Work of God.

[4] If anyone arrives at Vigils after the Gloria of Psalm Ninety-Four (which for this reason we wish to be said quite slowly and deliberately), he is not to stand in his usual rank in choir, [5] but last of all or in the place set apart by the abbot for the negligent, so that they may be seen by him and by all [6] until at the completion of the Work of God they make penance by public satisfaction.

[7] The reason we have judged that they should stand in the last place or apart is so that, being seen by all, they will amend out of shame: [8] for if they remained outside the oratory there might be some who would go back to bed and sleep; or else sit outside and spend their time in idle story–telling and *give occasion to the evil one* (EPHESIANS 4:27; I TIMOTHY 5:14). [9] Instead they are to come in, so that they do not lose everything and may amend for the future.

[10] But at the day hours, those who do not arrive at the Work of God until after the verse and the Gloria of the first psalm which is said after the verse, must stand, as was said above, in the last place: [11] nor may they presume to join the choir in psalmody until they have made satisfaction, unless the abbot permits it by giving his pardon: [12] but even so, satisfaction is to be made for this.

(RM 73:8-10)

[13] Ad mensam autem qui ante versu non occurrerit, ut simul omnes dicant versu et orent et sub uno omnes accedant ad mensam, [14] qui per neglegentiam suam aut vitio non occurrerit, usque secunda vice pro hoc corripiatur; [15] si denuo non emendaverit, non permittatur ad mensae communis participationem, [16] sed sequestratus a consortio omnium reficiat solus, sublata ei portione sua vinum, usque ad satisfactionem et emendationem. [17] Similiter autem patiatur qui et ad illum versum non fuerit praesens qui post cibum dicitur.

[18] Et ne quis praesumat ante statutam horam vel postea quicquam cibi aut potus praesumere; [19] sed et cui offertur aliquid a priore et accipere renuit, hora qua desideraverit hoc quod prius recusavit aut aliud, omnino nihil percipiat usque ad emendationem congruam.

(RM 14:17, 20-24; 13:60-61)

XLIV DE HIS QUI EXCOMMUNICANTUR, QUOMODO SATISFACIANT

[1] Qui pro gravibus culpis ab oratorio et a mensa excommunicantur, hora qua opus Dei in oratorio percelebratur, ante fores oratorii prostratus iaceat nihil dicens, [2] nisi tantum posito in terra capite, stratus pronus omnium de oratorio exeuntium pedibus; [3] et hoc tamdiu faciat usque dum abbas iudicaverit satisfactum esse.

Mar 23; July 23; Nov 22

[13] But if at table someone **has not arrived before** the verse, **so that all may together say the verse, pray, and sit down at table;** [14] he who through his own negligence or fault has not arrived is to be corrected once or twice: [15] If after this he does not amend, he will not be permitted to share the common table; [16] rather he is to be sequestered from the company of all to eat alone; and his portion of wine is to be withheld from him until he makes satisfaction and amends. [17] And the same is to be undergone by anyone who is not present at the verse which is said after meals.

[18] And no one may presume to take any food or drink before or after the appointed hour; [19] if, however, someone is offered something by the superior and refuses it, and then afterwards desires what he had rejected or something else, he is to receive nothing whatever until he has made suitable amends.

Mar 24; July 24; Nov 23

CHAPTER 44: THOSE WHO ARE EXCOMMUNICATED: HOW THEY ARE TO MAKE SATISFACTION

[1] He who for more serious faults has been excommunicated from both the oratory and the table is, at the end of the hour for the celebration of the Work of God, to cast himself prostrate before the entrance to the oratory, saying nothing: [2] without asking anything, he is to lie face down, prone on the ground at the feet of all as they leave the oratory; [3] and he is to do this until the abbot judges that satisfaction has been made.

[4] Qui dum iussus ab abbate venerit, volvat se ipsius abbatis deinde omnium vestigiis ut orent pro ipso, [5] et tunc, si iusserit abbas, recipiatur in choro vel in ordine quo abbas decreverit; [6] ita sane ut psalmum aut lectionem vel aliud quid non praesumat in oratorio imponere nisi iterum abbas iubeat; [7] et omnibus horis, dum percompletur opus Dei, proiciat se in terra in loco quo stat, [8] et sic satisfaciat usque dum ei iubeat iterum abbas ut quiescat iam ab hac satisfactione.

[9] Qui vero pro levibus culpis excommunicantur tantum a mensa, in oratorio satisfaciant usque ad iussionem abbatis; [10] hoc perficiant usque dum benedicat et dicat: "Sufficit!"

XLV DE HIS QUI FALLUNTUR IN ORATORIO

[1] Si quis dum pronuntiat psalmum, responsorium, antiphonam vel lectionem fallitus fuerit, nisi satisfactione ibi coram omnibus humiliatus fuerit, maiori vindictae subiaceat, [2] quippe qui noluit humilitate corrigere quod neglegentia deliquit. [3] Infantes autem pro tali culpa vapulent.

[4] **When he then receives the abbot's order, he is to prostrate himself first at abbot's feet, then at the feet of all so that they may** pray for him. [5] **And then, if the abbot so orders, he may be received back into choir, but in the rank the abbot assigns:** [6] **and he should** not **presume to** lead **a psalm, a** reading **or anything else in the** oratory **unless the abbot again commands it:** [7] **additionally, at every hour that the Work of God is completed he is to prostrate himself on the ground in the place where he stands;** [8] **and he thus makes satisfaction until the abbot again commands him to cease from this satisfaction.**

[9] **Those who for** lesser faults are excommunicated only from the table **are to** make satisfaction in the oratory until the abbot **gives the order:** [10] **they do this until he gives his blessing and says: "It is enough."**

Mar 25; July 25; Nov 24

CHAPTER 45: THOSE WHO MAKE MISTAKES IN THE ORATORY

[1] **If anyone makes a mistake while reciting a psalm, responsory, antiphon, or lesson and does not make satisfaction there before all by humbling himself, he is to be subjected to greater punishment,** [2] **for not correcting through humility what he did wrong through negligence.** [3] Children, however, are to be whipped for such faults.

XLVI DE HIS QUI IN ALIIS QUIBUSLIBET REBUS DELINQUUNT

[1] Si quis dum in labore quovis, in coquina, in cellario, in ministerio, in pistrino, in horto, in arte aliqua dum laborat, vel in quocumque loco, aliquid deliquerit, [2] aut fregerit quippiam aut perdiderit, vel aliud quid excesserit ubiubi, [3] et non veniens continuo ante abbatem vel congregationem ipse ultro satisfecerit et prodiderit delictum suum, [4] dum per alium cognitum fuerit, maiori subiaceat emendationi.

[5] Si animae vero peccati causa fuerit latens, tantum abbati aut spiritalibus senioribus patefaciat, [6] qui sciat curare et sua et aliena vulnera, non detegere et publicare.

(RM 31:1, 7-9; 46:1-2)

XLVII DE SIGNIFICANDA HORA OPERIS DEI

[1] Nuntianda hora operis Dei dies noctesque sit cura abbatis: aut ipse nuntiare aut tali sollicito fratri iniungat hanc curam, ut omnia horis competentibus compleantur. [2] Psalmos autem vel antiphonas post abbatem ordine suo quibus iussum fuerit imponant. [3] Cantare autem et legere non praesumat nisi qui potest ipsud officium implere ut aedificentur audientes; [4] quod cum humilitate et gravitate et tremore fiat, et cui iusserit abbas.

CHAPTER 46: THOSE WHO OFFEND IN OTHER MATTERS

[1] If someone while laboring at any kind of work, whether in the kitchen, in the cellar, while serving, in the bakery, in the garden, at any craft, or in any place, commits any fault [2] or breaks or loses something, or fails in any way whatever; [3] and if he does not immediately go before the abbot or the community and of his own accord make satisfaction and admit his fault: [4] if this is made known by means of another, he is to be subjected to more severe correction.

[5] If, however, the cause of the sin is hidden in the soul, he is to reveal it only to the abbot or to spiritual seniors, [6] who know how to heal both their own wounds and those of others without exposing them or making them public.

CHAPTER 47: ANNOUNCING THE HOURS FOR THE WORK OF GOD

[1] Announcing the hour for the Work of God day and night is the abbot's responsibility, whether he gives the signal himself or assigns this responsibility to a conscientious brother; so that all things may be completed at the appropriate hours. [2] Psalms and antiphons, however, are to be led after the abbot according to rank by those he appoints. [3] And no one may presume to sing or read unless he can fulfil this office by edifying his hearers: [4] this is to be done with humility, seriousness and reverence, and as the abbot orders.

(RM 50:1, 7, 39-42, 53-56, 62-64)

XLVIII DE OPERA MANUUM COTIDIANA

[1] Otiositas inimica est animae, et ideo certis temporibus occupari debent fratres in labore manuum, certis iterum horis in lectione divina.

[2] Ideoque hac dispositione credimus utraque tempore ordinari: [3] id est ut a Pascha usque kalendas Octobres a mane exeuntes a prima usque hora paene quarta laborent quod necessarium fuerit; [4] ab hora autem quarta usque hora qua sextam agent lectioni vacent; [5] post sextam autem surgentes a mensa pausent in lecta sua cum omni silentio, aut forte qui voluerit legere sibi sic legat ut alium non inquietet; [6] et agatur nona temperius mediante octava hora, et iterum quod faciendum est operentur usque ad vesperam.

[7] Si autem necessitas loci aut paupertas exegerit ut ad fruges recolligendas per se occupentur, non contristentur, [8] quia tunc vere monachi sunt si labore manuum suarum vivunt, sicut et patres nostri et apostoli. [9] Omnia tamen mensurate fiant propter pusillanimes.

CHAPTER 48: DAILY MANUAL LABOR

[1] Idleness is the enemy of the soul; and therefore the brothers should be occupied at certain times in manual labor, and at certain other hours in sacred reading.

[2] We therefore believe that the times for each may be ordered thus: [3] from Easter to the first of October, on coming out after Prime they are to labor at whatever is necessary from the first until about the fourth hour; [4] from the fourth hour until about the time they say Sext they are to devote themselves to reading; [5] after Sext upon arising from table they are to rest on their beds in complete silence, or if anyone wishes to read to himself he may read, but without disturbing the others; [6] and None is to be performed rather early at the middle of the eighth hour; then they are again to work at whatever needs to be done until Vespers.

[7] If, however, local necessity or poverty require that they themselves are occupied with gathering the harvest, they should not be saddened; [8] for they are then truly monks when they live by the labor of their hands, as did our fathers and the apostles. [9] But everything is to be done with proper measure on account of the fainthearted.

(RM 50:10, 14-15)

[10] **A** kalendas **autem** Octobres **usque caput quadragesimae, usque in hora secunda plena** lectioni vacent; [11] **hora secunda agatur tertia, et usque nona omnes in opus suum laborent quod eis iniungitur;** [12] facto autem primo signo nonae horae, deiungant ab opera sua singuli et sint parati dum secundum signum pulsaverit. [13] Post refectionem autem vacent lectionibus suis aut psalmis.

[14] **In quadragesimae vero diebus, a mane usque tertia plena vacent lectionibus suis, et usque decima hora plena operentur quod eis iniungitur.** [15] **In quibus diebus quadragesimae accipiant omnes singulos codices de bibliotheca, quos per ordinem ex integro legant;** [16] **qui codices in caput quadragesimae dandi sunt.**

[17] **Ante omnia sane deputentur unus aut duo** seniores qui circumeant monasterium horis quibus vacant **fratres lectioni,** [18] **et videant ne forte inveniatur frater acediosus qui vacat otio aut** fabulis et non est intentus lectioni, et non solum sibi inutilis est, sed etiam alios distollit: [19] hic talis si— quod absit—repertus fuerit, corripiatur semel et secundo; [20] si non emendaverit, correptioni regulari subiaceat taliter ut ceteri timeant. [21] Neque frater ad fratrem iungatur horis incompetentibus.

Mar 29; July 29; Nov 28

10 From the first of October **until the beginning of Lent they are to** devote themselves to reading **until the end of the second hour:** 11 at the second hour Terce is to be said, and until None all are to labor at their appointed work. 12 But at the first signal for the hour of None all are to cease from their work, and prepare for the sounding of the second signal. 13 After the meal they are to devote themselves to their reading or to the psalms.

14 In the days of Lent, however, from morning until the end of the third hour they should devote themselves to their reading, and afterwards work until the end of the tenth hour at their assigned tasks 15 In these days of Lent each is to receive a book from the library, to be completely read straight through: 16 these books are to be given out at the beginning of Lent.

17 Above all, one or two seniors should be deputed to make the rounds of monastery at the hours when the brothers are devoted to reading; 18 and they are to see that there is not found any brother giving in to *acedia,* who devotes himself to idleness or idle story-telling, and does not apply himself to his reading: he is thus not only useless to himself, but a distraction to others. 19 If one is found (may it not happen!) he is to be corrected once and then a second time, 20 and if he does not amend he is to be subjected to the chastisement of the Rule, in such a way as to inspire fear in the rest. 21 And no brother may associate with another brother at inappropriate hours.

(RM 50:75-78)

²² Dominico item die lectioni vacent omnes, excepto his qui variis officiis deputati sunt. ²³ Si quis vero ita neglegens et desidiosus fuerit ut non velit aut non possit meditare aut legere, iniungatur ei opus quod faciat, ut non vacet.

²⁴ Fratribus infirmis aut delicatis talis opera aut ars iniungatur ut nec otiosi sint nec violentia laboris opprimantur aut effugentur. ²⁵ Quorum imbecillitas ab abbate consideranda est.

(RM 51:1-3; 52:1-2, 6; 53:12-15)

XLIX DE QUADRAGESIMAE OBSERVATIONE

¹ Licet omni tempore vita monachi quadragesimae debet observationem habere, ² tamen, quia paucorum est ista virtus, ideo suademus istis diebus quadragesimae omni puritate vitam suam custodire omnes pariter, ³ et neglegentias aliorum temporum his diebus sanctis diluere. ⁴ Quod tunc digne fit si ab omnibus vitiis temperamus, orationi cum fletibus, lectioni et compunctioni cordis atque abstinentiae operam damus. ⁵ Ergo his diebus augeamus nobis aliquid solito pensu servitutis nostrae, orationes peculiares, ciborum et potus abstinentiam, ⁶ ut unusquisque super mensuram sibi indictam aliquid propria voluntate *cum gaudio Sancti Spiritus* offerat Deo, ⁷ id est subtrahat corpori suo de cibo, de potu, de somno, de loquacitate, de scurrilitate, et cum spiritalis *desiderii* gaudio sanctum *Pascha* exspectet.

22 On Sunday all are to devote themselves to reading except those assigned various duties. 23 But if anyone is so negligent and lazy as to be unwilling or unable to meditate or read, he is to be given work to do so that he is not idle.

24 Brothers who are sick or weak are to be assigned such work or crafts that they will not be idle, and yet will not be oppressed by heavy labor and so driven away. 25 Such infirmities are to be taken into consideration by the abbot.

CHAPTER 49: THE OBSERVANCE OF LENT

1 Although at all times the life of a monk to be a Lenten observance, 2 yet since few have the strength for this we encourage all during these days of Lent to keep themselves in all purity of life, 3 and to wash away the neglected matters of other times during these holy days. 4 This we will do worthily do if we abstain from all vices and give ourselves to prayer with tears, reading, compunction of heart, and abstinence. 5 Therefore during these days let us augment somewhat our usual quota of service through private prayers and abstinence from food and drink, 6 so that each may offer, above his appointed measure and of his own free will, something to God *in the joy of the Holy Spirit* (I THESSALONAINS 1:6): 7 that is, by withholding from his body something of food, drink, sleep, excessive talking, ridiculing; and thus awaiting holy *Easter* with the joy of spiritual *desire* (*cf.* LUKE 22:15).

⁸ Hoc ipsud tamen quod unusquisque offerit abbati suo suggerat, et cum eius fiat oratione et voluntate, ⁹ quia quod sine permissione patris spiritalis fit, praesumptioni deputabitur et vanae gloriae, non mercedi. ¹⁰ Ergo cum voluntate abbatis omnia agenda sunt.

(RM 55:1, 4, 17-18; 56:1, 19)

L DE FRATRIBUS QUI LONGE AB ORATORIO LABORANT AUT IN VIA SUNT

¹ Fratres qui omnino longe sunt in labore et non possunt occurrere hora competenti ad oratorium— ² et abbas hoc perpendet, quia ita est— ³ agant ibidem opus Dei, ubi operantur, cum tremore divino flectentes genua. ⁴ Similiter, qui in itinere directi sunt, non eos praetereant horae constitutae, sed ut possunt agant sibi et servitutis pensum non neglegant reddere.

(RM 61:1-3)

LI DE FRATRIBUS QUI NON LONGE SATIS PROFICISCUNTUR

¹ Frater qui pro quovis responso dirigitur et ea die speratur reverti ad monasterium, non praesumat foris manducare, etiam si omnino rogetur a quovis, ² nisi forte ei ab abbate suo praecipiatur. ³ Quod si aliter fecerit, excommunicetur.

8 Everyone is, however, is to make known to his abbot what he offers, and do it with his prayer and according to his will, 9 because what is done without permission of the spiritual father will be attributed to presumption and vainglory, and will merit no reward. 10 Therefore everything is to be according to the will of the abbot.

Apr 1; Aug 1; Dec 1

CHAPTER 50: BROTHERS WHO WORK FAR FROM THE ORATORY OR ARE ON A JOURNEY

1 Brothers who work some distance away and are not able to come at the proper hour to the oratory 2 (and the abbot judges that this is the case) 3 should perform the Work of God there where they are working, bending their knees in reverent awe. 4 Similarly, those sent on a journey should not allow the appointed hours to pass them by; instead, insofar as they can, they should perform them there, thus not neglecting to offer their quota of service.

Apr 2; Aug 2; Dec 2

CHAPTER 51: BROTHERS WHO ARE NOT GOING FAR AWAY

1 A brother who is sent out for some reason and expects to return that same day to the monastery may not presume to eat outside, even if someone asks him to, 2 unless he has been given permission by his abbot. 3 If he acts otherwise he is to be excommunicated.

(RM 68:1-4; cf. 53:64-65)

LII DE ORATORIO
MONASTERII

[1] Oratorium hoc sit quod dicitur, nec ibi quicquam aliud geratur aut condatur. [2] Expleto opere Dei, omnes cum summo silentio exeant, et habeatur reverentia Deo, [3] ut frater qui forte sibi peculiariter vult orare non impediatur alterius improbitate. [4] Sed et si aliter vult sibi forte secretius orare, simpliciter intret et oret, non in clamosa voce, sed in lacrimis et intentione cordis. [5] Ergo qui simile opus non facit, non permittatur explicito opere Dei remorari in oratorio, sicut dictum est, ne alius impedimentum patiatur.

(RM 71:1-2, 5-10; 65:1-9; 72:1-6; 79:1-2)

LIII DE HOSPITIBUS SUSCIPIENDIS

[1] Omnes supervenientes hospites tamquam Christus suscipiantur, quia ipse dicturus est: *Hospes fui et suscepistis me;* [2] et *omnibus* congruus honor exhibeatur, *maxime domesticis fidei* et peregrinis.

[3] Ut ergo nuntiatus fuerit hospes, occurratur ei a priore vel a fratribus cum omni officio caritatis, [4] et primitus orent pariter, et sic sibi socientur in pace. [5] Quod pacis osculum non prius offeratur nisi oratione praemissa, propter illusiones diabolicas.

CHAPTER 52: THE ORATORY OF THE MONASTERY

[1] The oratory is to be what it is called, and nothing else should be done or kept there. [2] When the Work of God is finished all should go out in complete silence and with reverence for God, [3] so that a brother who wishes to pray by himself will not be impeded by another's insensitivity. [4] But if he wishes to pray in solitude, he should enter to pray with simplicity, not in a loud voice but with tears and attentiveness of heart. [5] And therefore one who is not performing this work is not to be permitted to remain in the oratory after the Work of God, so that, as was said, no one else is impeded.

CHAPTER 53: THE RECEPTION OF GUESTS

[1] All guests who present themselves are to be received as Christ, for He will say: *I was a stranger and you took me in* (MATTHEW 25:35). [2] And *to everyone* fitting honor is to be shown, *especially to those of the household of faith* (GALATIANS 6:10) and to pilgrims.

[3] When, therefore, a guest is announced, he is to be met by the superior and the brothers with every ceremony of love: [4] thus first they are to pray together, and thus be united to one another in peace. [5] But this kiss of peace is not to be offered until prayer has first been said on account of the illusions of the devil.

⁶ In ipsa autem salutatione omnis exhibeatur humilitas omnibus venientibus sive discedentibus hospitibus: ⁷ inclinato capite vel prostrato omni corpore in terra, Christus in eis adoretur qui et suscipitur.

⁸ Suscepti autem hospites ducantur ad orationem et postea sedeat cum eis prior aut cui iusserit ipse. ⁹ Legatur coram hospite lex divina ut aedificetur, et post haec omnis ei exhibeatur humanitas.

¹⁰ Ieiunium a priore frangatur propter hospitem, nisi forte praecipuus sit dies ieiunii qui non possit violari; ¹¹ fratres autem consuetudines ieiuniorum prosequantur. ¹² Aquam in manibus abbas hospitibus det; ¹³ pedes hospitibus omnibus tam abbas quam cuncta congregatio lavet; ¹⁴ quibus lotis, hunc versum dicant: *Suscepimus, Deus, misericordiam tuam in medio templi tui.*

¹⁵ Pauperum et peregrinorum maxime susceptioni cura sollicite exhibeatur, quia in ipsis magis Christus suscipitur; nam divitum terror ipse sibi exigit honorem.

[6] And in this very salutation all humility is to be shown to all arriving or departing guests: [7] by bowing the head or prostrating the whole body on the ground Christ is to be adored in them just as he is received in them.

[8] And having been received the guests are to be led to prayer, and afterwards the superior or anyone he appoints is to sit with them. [9] The divine law is to be read to the guest for his edification, and afterwards all kindness is to be shown him.

[10] The superior is to break his fast for the sake of the guest, unless it happens to be a principal fast–day which cannot be broken: [11] the brothers, however, are to follow their customary fast. [12] Water is to be poured on the hands of the guests by the abbot, [13] and the feet of all guests are to be washed by the abbot and the whole community. [14] After the washing they are to say this verse: *We have received your mercy, O God, in the midst of your temple* (PSALM 48:10).

[15] In the reception of the poor and of pilgrims the greatest care and solicitude should be shown, because in them Christ is more especially received: For the very awe we have of the rich insures that they receive honor.

(RM 16:45-46; 79:1-2)

[16] Coquina abbatis et hospitum super se sit, ut, incertis horis supervenientes hospites, qui numquam desunt monasterio, non inquietentur fratres. [17] In qua coquina ad annum ingrediantur duo fratres qui ipsud officium bene impleant. [18] Quibus, ut indigent, solacia administrentur, ut absque murmuratione serviant, et iterum, quando occupationem minorem habent, exeant ubi eis imperatur in opera. [19] Et non solum ipsis, sed et in omnibus officiis monasterii ista sit consideratio, [20] ut quando indigent solacia accommodentur eis, et iterum quando vacant oboediant imperatis.

[21] Item et cellam hospitum habeat assignatam frater cuius animam timor Dei possidet; [22] ubi sint lecti strati sufficienter. Et domus Dei a sapientibus et sapienter administretur.

[23] Hospitibus autem cui non praecipitur ullatenus societur neque colloquatur; [24] sed si obviaverit aut viderit, salutatis humiliter, ut diximus, et petita benedictione pertranseat, dicens sibi non licere colloqui cum hospite.

[16] The kitchen for the abbot and guests is to be set apart by itself so that guests who arrive at uncertain hours (and who are never lacking in a monastery) may not disturb the brothers. [17] In this kitchen each year two brothers are to be placed who can fulfill this duty properly. [18] These, if they require it, are to be offered help so that they may serve without murmuring; and when, on the other hand, they are occupied with less, they are to go out wherever they are commanded to work. [19] And not only to them, but in all the duties of the monastery this same consideration is to be shown: [20] that is, when help is required it is given to them; and again, when they are free they obey what they are commanded to do.

[21] And the guest–house is to be assigned to a brother whose soul is possessed by the fear of God: [22] sufficient beds should be provided there. And the house of God is to be wisely administered by wise men.

[23] Guests, however, are not to be associated with or conversed with for any reason by one not assigned to do so: [24] instead, if he happens to meet or see them, he is to humbly greet them as we have said; and as he asks their blessing he is to continue on, saying that he is not permitted to talk with a guest.

LIV SI DEBEAT MONACHUS LITTERAS VEL ALIQUID SUSCIPERE

[1] Nullatenus liceat monacho neque a parentibus suis neque a quoquam hominum nec sibi invicem litteras, eulogias vel quaelibet munuscula accipere aut dare sine praecepto abbatis. [2] Quod si etiam a parentibus suis ei quicquam directum fuerit non praesumat suscipere illud, nisi prius indicatum fuerit abbati.

[3] Quod si iusserit suscipi, in abbatis sit potestate cui illud iubeat dari, [4] et non contristetur frater cui forte directum fuerat, *ut non detur occasio diabolo*. [5] Qui autem aliter praesumpserit, disciplinae regulari subiaceat.

(RM 81:1-8, 25-30)

LV DE VESTIARIO VEL CALCIARIO FRATRUM

[1] Vestimenta fratribus secundum locorum qualitatem ubi habitant vel aerum temperiem dentur, [2] quia in frigidis regionibus amplius indigetur, in calidis vero minus. [3] Haec ergo consideratio penes abbatem est. [4] Nos tamen mediocribus locis sufficere credimus monachis per singulos cucullam et tunicam—[5] cucullam in hieme villosam, in aestate puram aut vetustam—[6] et scapulare propter opera, indumenta pedum pedules et caligas.

CHAPTER 54: WHETHER A MONK MAY RECEIVE LETTERS OR ANYTHING ELSE

[1] For no reason is it permissible for a monk to receive from his parents or from any other person —not even the brethren—letters, blessed objects, or any little gifts of any kind; nor may he give them to others, without permission of the abbot. [2] For even if something is sent to him by his parents, he may not presume to receive it unless he has first indicated this to the abbot.

[3] If he orders it to be received, it is in the abbot's power to decide to whom it will be given; [4] and this is not to sadden the brother to whom it was sent, *so that occasion is not given to the devil* (EPHESIANS 4:27; I TIMOTHY 5:14). [5] But one who presumes to act otherwise is to be subjected to the discipline of the Rule.

CHAPTER 55: THE CLOTHING AND FOOTWEAR OF THE BROTHERS

[1] Clothing is to be given to the brothers according to the nature of the place where they live and according to its climate; [2] for in cold regions more is required and in warm regions less. [3] This therefore is for the abbot to consider. [4] We believe, however, that in temperate places a cowl and a tunic will suffice for each monk, [5] the cowl to be of shaggy wool in winter, but in summer thin or worn; [6] also a scapular for work, and to cover their feet stockings and shoes.

[7] De quarum rerum omnium colore aut grossitudine non causentur monachi, sed quales inveniri possunt in provincia qua degunt aut quod vilius comparari possit. [8] Abbas autem de mensura provideat ut non sint curta ipsa vestimenta utentibus ea, sed mensurata.

[9] Accipientes nova, vetera semper reddant in praesenti reponenda in vestiario propter pauperes. [10] Sufficit enim monacho duas tunicas et duas cucullas habere propter noctes et propter lavare ipsas res; [11] iam quod supra fuerit superfluum est, amputari debet. [12] Et pedules et quodcumque est vetere reddant dum accipiunt novum.

[13] Femoralia hi qui in via diriguntur de vestario accipiant, quae revertentes lota ibi restituant. [14] Et cucullae et tunicae sint aliquanto a solito quas habent modice meliores; quas exeuntes in via accipiant de vestiario et revertentes restituant.

(RM 81:31-33)

[15] Stramenta autem lectorum sufficiant matta, sagum et lena, et capitale. [16] Quae tamen lecta frequenter ab abbate scrutinanda sunt propter opus peculiare, ne inveniatur; [17] et si cui inventum fuerit quod ab abbate non accepit, gravissimae disciplinae subiaceat. [18] Et ut hoc vitium peculiaris radicitus amputetur, dentur ab abbate omnia quae sunt necessaria,

7 Concerning the color or coarseness of all these things the monks should not complain; rather, whatever can be easily obtained in the province where they live or can be bought cheaply they should use. 8 The abbot is to see to the measurements, so that these garments are not too short for those who use them, but rather are properly measured.

9 On receiving new clothes the old should always be returned at once, to be stored in the wardrobe for the poor. 10 For it is sufficient for a monk to have two tunics and two cowls, on account of night wear and on account of laundering these items; 11 anything beyond this is superfluous and is to be cut off. 12 And stockings and whatever else is old are to be returned when they receive new things.

13 Underclothing for those who are sent on a journey is to be received from the wardrobe, which those who return are to wash and replace. 14 Their cowls and tunics should also be somewhat better than their usual wear: those leaving on a journey are to receive these from the wardrobe and those returning are to replace them.

Apr 8; Aug 8; Dec 8

15 For bedding a mat, a heavy and a light blanket, and a pillow suffice. 16 These beds are to be frequently inspected by the abbot so that personal possessions are not found there; 17 and if anyone is found with something he has not received from the abbot, he is to be subjected to the most severe discipline. 18 And so as to cut out this vice of personal ownership at the roots, the abbot is to give out everything that is necessary:

[19] id est cuculla, tunica, pedules, caligas, bracile, cultellum, graphium, acum, mappula, tabulas, ut omnis auferatur necessitatis excusatio.
[20] A quo tamen abbate semper consideretur illa sententia Actuum Apostolorum, quia *dabatur singulis prout cuique opus erat.* [21] Ita ergo et abbas consideret infirmitates indigentium, non malum voluntatem invidentium; [22] in omnibus tamen iudiciis suis Dei retributionem cogitet.

(RM 84:1-2)

LVI DE MENSA ABBATIS

[1] Mensa abbatis cum hospitibus et peregrinis sit semper. [2] Quotiens tamen minus sunt hospites, quos vult de fratribus vocare in ipsius sit potestate. [3] Seniore tamen uno aut duo semper cum fratribus dimittendum propter disciplinam.

(RM 85:2-6; 87:24)

LVII DE ARTIFICIBUS MONASTERII

[1] Artifices si sunt in monasterio cum omni humilitate faciant ipsas artes, si permiserit abbas. [2] Quod si aliquis ex eis extollitur pro scientia artis suae, eo quod videatur aliquid conferre monasterio, [3] hic talis erigatur ab ipsa arte et denuo per eam non transeat, nisi forte humiliato ei iterum abbas iubeat.

[4] Si quid vero ex operibus artificum venumdandum est, videant ipsi per quorum manus transigenda sint ne aliquam fraudem praesumant.

[19] that is, cowl, tunic, stockings, shoes, belt, knife, stylus, needle, handkerchief, and writing tablets; so that every excuse based on necessity is removed. [20] However the abbot must always take into consideration this sentence from the Acts of the Apostles: *They gave to each one according to his need* (ACTS 4:35). [21] Therefore the abbot is also to take into consideration the weaknesses of those in need, not the ill-will of the envious: [22] nevertheless, in all his decisions he is to ponder the retribution of God.

Apr 9; Aug 9; Dec 9

CHAPTER 56: THE TABLE OF THE ABBOT

[1] The table of the abbot should always be with guests and pilgrims. [2] Whenever there are few guests it is within his power to invite any of the brothers he wishes. [3] He is, however, always to leave one or two seniors with the brothers for the sake of discipline.

Apr 10; Aug 10; Dec 10

CHAPTER 57: THE CRAFTSMEN OF THE MONASTERY

[1] If there are craftsmen in the monastery, they are to practice their crafts in all humility if the abbot permits it. [2] But if any one of them becomes conceited because of his knowledge of his craft, determining that he thus confers something on the monastery, [3] he is to be taken from that craft and not permitted to exercise it again, unless having humbled himself, the abbot orders him back to it.

[4] If any products of the craftsmen are to be sold, care should be taken that those by whose hands the transaction takes place do not presume to practice any fraud.

[5] Memorentur semper Ananiae et Saphirae, ne forte mortem quam illi in corpore pertulerunt, [6] hanc isti vel omnes qui aliquam fraudem de rebus monasterii fecerint in anima patiantur.

[7] In ipsis autem pretiis non surripiat avaritiae malum, [8] sed semper aliquantulum vilius detur quam ab aliis saecularibus dari potest, [9] ut in omnibus glorificetur Deus.

LVIII   DE DISCIPLINA
SUSCIPIENDORUM FRATRUM

[1] Noviter veniens quis ad conversationem, non ei facilis tribuatur ingressus, [2] sed sicut ait apostolus: *Probate spiritus si ex Deo sunt.* [3] Ergo si veniens perseveraverit pulsans et illatas sibi iniurias et difficultatem ingressus post quattuor aut quinque dies visus fuerit patienter portare et persistere petitioni suae, [4] adnuatur ei ingressus et sit in cella hospitum paucis diebus. [5] Postea autem sit in cella noviciorum ubi meditent et manducent et dormiant.

[6] Et senior eis talis deputetur qui aptus sit ad lucrandas animas, qui super eos omnino curiose intendat. [7] Et sollicitudo sit si revera Deum quaerit, si sollicitus est ad opus Dei, ad oboedientiam, ad opprobria. [8] Praedicentur ei omnia dura et aspera per quae itur ad Deum.

[5] **They are always to** remember Ananias and Sapphira (ACTS 5:1-11), **lest the death which those two incurred in the body be suffered in their souls** [6] **and those of all who practice any fraud in business of the monastery.**

[7] **In establishing their prices the evil of** avarice must not creep in: [8] **instead, the goods should always be sold for a little less than those living in the world are able to charge,** [9] *so that in everything God may be glorified* (I PETER 4:11).

Apr 11; Aug 11; Dec 11

CHAPTER 58: THE DISCIPLINE OF RECEIVING BROTHERS

[1] **One** newly **arriving to this way of life is not to be granted an easy entrance;** [2] **rather, as the apostle says,** *Test the spirits, whether they are from God* (I JOHN 4:1). [3] **Therefore if the one who comes perseveres in knocking and appears to patiently endure injuries done him and difficulties concerning his entrance for four or five days, and if he still persists in his petition,** [4] **entrance is to be granted him, and he is to stay in the guest-house for a few days.** [5] **But after this he is to stay in the novitiate, where he is to meditate, eat, and sleep.**

[6] **And to him a senior is to be deputed who is skilled at winning souls, who will watch over him with all care.** [7] **And it should be** eagerly ascertained **whether he truly seeks God, whether he is eager for the Work of God, for obedience, and for humbling experiences.** [8] **To him should be** proclaimed **everything of the roughness and pain by which we journey towards God.**

[9] Si promiserit de stabilitate sua perseverantia, post duorum mensuum circulum legatur ei haec regula per ordinem [10] et dicatur ei: Ecce lex sub qua militare vis; si potes observare, ingredere; si vero non potes, liber discede. [11] Si adhuc steterit, tunc ducatur in supradictam cellam noviciorum et iterum probetur in omni patientia. [12] Et post sex mensuum circuitum legatur ei regula, ut sciat ad quod ingreditur. [13] Et si adhuc stat, post quattuor menses iterum relegatur ei eadem regula. [14] Et si habita secum deliberatione promiserit se omnia custodire et cuncta sibi imperata servare, tunc suscipiatur in congregatione, [15] sciens et lege regulae constitutum quod ei ex illa die non liceat egredi de monasterio, [16] nec collum excutere de sub iugo regulae quem sub tam morosam deliberationem licuit aut excusare aut suscipere.

[17] Suscipiendus autem in oratorio coram omnibus promittat de stabilitate sua et conversatione morum suorum et oboedientia, [18] coram Deo et sanctis eius, ut si aliquando aliter fecerit, ab eo se damnandum sciat quem irridit.

[19] De qua promissione sua faciat petitionem ad nomen sanctorum quorum reliquiae ibi sunt et abbatis praesentis.

⁹ If he promises perseverance in his stability, after a period of two months this Rule is to be read to him straight through ¹⁰ and then he is to be told: **"Behold the law under which you wish to fight: if you are able to observe it, enter; if you are not able, freely depart."** ¹¹ If he still stands firm, he is to be taken to the novitiate described above and again tested in all patience. ¹² After a period of six months, the Rule is to be read to him again, so that he knows what he is entering. ¹³ And if he still stands firm, after four months the same Rule is to be read to him once again. ¹⁴ And if, having deliberated within himself, he promises to keep everything and to submit in all that he is ordered, then he is to be received into the community ¹⁵ knowing that the law of the Rule establishes that from that day he is no longer free to depart from the monastery ¹⁶ nor remove his neck from beneath the yoke of the Rule which after such prolonged deliberation he was free to either refuse or to accept.

Apr 11; Aug 11; Dec 11

¹⁷ The one being received is to make in the oratory before all a promise of his stability, his faithfulness to the way of life, and obedience. ¹⁸ This is done before God and His saints so that if he ever acts otherwise he will know Who it is that condemns him—the One whom he mocks.

¹⁹ Concerning his promise he is to make a petition in the name of the saints whose relics are there, and of the abbot who is present.

20 **Quam** petitionem manu sua **scribat, aut certe, si
non scit litteras, alter ab eo rogatus scribat et ille
novicius signum faciat et** manu sua **eam** super altare
ponat. 21 **Quam dum imposuerit, incipiat ipse**
novicius **mox hunc versum:** Suscipe me, Domine,
secundum **eloquium** tuum et vivam, et ne confundas
me ab exspectatione mea. 22 **Quem versum omnis
congregatio tertio respondeat, adiungentes Gloria
Patri.** 23 **Tunc ille frater novicius prosternatur
singulorum pedibus ut orent pro eo, et iam ex illa
die in congregatione reputetur.**

24 **Res, si quas habet, aut eroget prius pauperibus
aut facta sollemniter** donatione conferat monasterio,
nihil sibi reservans ex omnibus, 25 **quippe qui ex
illo die nec proprii corporis potestatem se
habiturum scit.** 26 **Mox ergo in oratorio exuatur
rebus propriis quibus vestitus est et induatur rebus
monasterii.** 27 **Illa autem vestimenta quibus exutus
est reponantur in vestiario conservanda,** 28 **ut si
aliquando** suadenti diabolo **consenserit ut egrediatur
de monasterio—quod absit—tunc exutus rebus
monasterii proiciatur.** 29 **Illam tamen petitionem
eius, quam** desuper altare abbas tulit, **non recipiat,
sed in monasterio reservetur.**

²⁰ This petition he is to write with his own hand: or if he is illiterate, another is to write it at his request; and the novice is then to make his sign on it with his own hand and place it upon the altar. ²¹ When he has placed it there, the novice himself is to begin this verse: *Uphold me, Lord, according to your word, and I shall live; let not my hope be put to shame* (PSALM 119:116). ²² This verse is to be repeated by the whole community three times, adding to it a 'Glory be.' ²³ Then the brother novice is to prostrate himself at the feet of all, so that they may pray for him: and from that day he is to be considered part of the community.

Apr 12; Aug 12; Dec 12

²⁴ If he has any possessions he should either first bestow them on the poor, or by a solemn deed of gift donate them to the monastery, keeping nothing for himself; ²⁵ knowing that from that day onwards he will not even have power concerning his own body. ²⁶ Immediately afterwards in the oratory he is to be stripped of his own garments which he is wearing, and be clothed in those of the monastery. ²⁷ Those garments which are taken from him are to be placed in the clothes-room and kept there, ²⁸ so that if ever by the persuasion of the devil he consents (may it never happen!) to leave the monastery, he may be stripped of the things of the monastery and cast forth. ²⁹ The petition, however, which the abbot received on the altar will not be given back to him, but will be kept in the monastery.

(RM 90:5-6, 42-47)

LIX DE FILIIS NOBILIUM AUT PAUPERUM QUI OFFERUNTUR

[1] Si quis forte de nobilibus offerit filium suum Deo in monasterio, si ipse puer minor aetate est, parentes eius faciant petitionem quam supra diximus [2] et cum oblatione ipsam petitionem et manum pueri involvant in palla altaris, et sic eum offerant.

[3] De rebus autem suis, aut in praesenti petitione promittant sub iureiurando quia numquam per se, numquam per suffectam personam nec quolibet modo ei aliquando aliquid dant aut tribuunt occasionem habendi; [4] vel certe si hoc facere noluerint et aliquid offerre volunt in eleemosynam monasterio pro mercede sua, [5] faciant ex rebus quas dare volunt monasterio donationem, reservato sibi, si ita voluerint, usufructu. [6] Atque ita omnia obstruantur ut nulla suspicio remaneat puero per quam deceptus perire possit—quod absit—quod experimento didicimus.

[7] Similiter autem et pauperiores faciant. [8] Qui vero ex toto nihil habent, simpliciter petitionem faciant et cum oblatione offerant filium suum coram testibus.

Apr 13; Aug 13; Dec 13

CHAPTER 59: SONS OF THE NOBILITY OR THE POOR WHO ARE OFFERED

[1] If a member of the nobility offers his son to God in the monastery and if the child is of tender years, his parents are to make the petition of which we spoke above; [2] and, together with the offerings, they are to wrap that petition and the hand of the child in the altar-cloth, and so offer him.

[3] With regard to his property in the same petition they are to promise under oath that they will never, either directly, through an intermediary, or in any other way give him anything or the means of having anything: [4] or else, if they are unwilling to do this and wish to give something as an benefaction to the monastery to win their reward, [5] they are to make a donation to the monastery of the property they wish to give, reserving to themselves, if they so wish the revenues. [6] And thus let every way be blocked, so that no sort of expectation will remain by which the child might be deceived and perish (may it never happen!), which experience has taught us may happen.

[7] Those who are poorer are to do the same. [8] But those who have nothing whatever are to simply make the petition and offer their son along with the offerings before witnesses.

(RM 83:3-7, 10-11)

LX DE SACERDOTIBUS QUI FORTE VOLUERINT IN MONASTERIO HABITARE

[1] Si quis de ordine sacerdotum in monasterio se suscipi rogaverit, non quidem citius ei assentiatur. [2] Tamen, si omnino persteterit in hac supplicatione, sciat se omnem regulae disciplinam servaturum, [3] nec aliquid ei relaxabitur, ut sit sicut scriptum est: *Amice, ad quod venisti?* [4] Concedatur ei tamen post abbatem stare et benedicere aut missas tenere, si tamen iusserit ei abbas; [5] sin alias, ullatenus aliqua praesumat, sciens se disciplinae regulari subditum, et magis humilitatis exempla omnibus det. [6] Et si forte ordinationis aut alicuius rei causa fuerit in monasterio, [7] illum locum attendat quando ingressus est in monasterio, non illum qui ei pro reverentia sacerdotii concessus est.

[8] Clericorum autem si quis eodem desiderio monasterio sociari voluerit, loco mediocri collocentur; [9] et ipsi tamen si promittunt de observatione regulae vel propria stabilitate.

CHAPTER 60: PRIESTS WHO WISH TO LIVE IN THE MONASTERY

[1] If anyone ordained to the priesthood asks to be received into the monastery, assent should not be granted him too quickly. [2] But if he definitively persists in this request, he must know that he will have to keep all the discipline of the Rule [3] and that nothing will be relaxed in his favor, for it is written: *Friend, for what have you come* (MATTHEW 26:50)? [4] Nevertheless, it is permitted him to stand in the next place after the abbot, to give the blessing, and to celebrate Mass if the abbot tells him to do so: [5] without this he is not to presume anything whatever, knowing that he is subject to the discipline of the Rule and that he should moreover give an example of humility to all. [6] And if there arises a question of an appointment or of other matters in the monastery, [7] he is to regard as his place that which corresponds to his time of entry in the monastery, and not that which was conceded him out of reverence for the priesthood.

[8] With regard to clerics, if one of them has a similar desire and wishes membership in the monastery, he is to be placed in a middle rank; [9] and this only if they promise observance of the Rule and stability.

(RM 79: 23-28)

LXI DE MONACHIS PEREGRINIS, QUALITER SUSCIPIANTUR

[1] Si quis monachus peregrinus de longinquis provinciis supervenerit, si pro hospite voluerit habitare in monasterio [2] et contentus est consuetudinem loci quam invenerit, et non forte superfluitate sua perturbat monasterium, [3] sed simpliciter contentus est quod invenerit, suscipiatur quanto tempore cupit. [4] Si qua sane rationabiliter et cum humilitate caritatis reprehendit aut ostendit, tractet abbas prudenter ne forte pro hoc ipsud eum Dominus direxerit.

[5] Si vero postea voluerit stabilitatem suam firmare, non renuatur talis voluntas, et maxime quia tempore hospitalitatis potuit eius vita dinosci.

(cf. RM 83:17-22)

[6] Quod si superfluus aut vitiosus inventus fuerit tempore hospitalitatis, non solum non debet sociari corpori monasterii, [7] verum etiam dicatur ei honeste ut discedat, ne eius miseria etiam alii vitientur.

[8] Quod si non fuerit talis qui mereatur proici, non solum si petierit suscipiatur congregationi sociandus, [9] verum etiam suadeatur ut stet, ut eius exemplo alii erudiantur, [10] et quia in omni loco uni Domino servitur, uni regi militatur. [11] Quem si etiam talem esse perspexerit abbas, liceat eum in superiori aliquantum constituere loco.

Apr 15; Aug 15; Dec 15

CHAPTER 61: HOW VISITING MONKS ARE RECEIVED

[1] If a pilgrim–monk arrives from distant provinces and wishes to stay as a guest in the monastery, [2] and if he is content with the customs of the place as he finds them and does not by fussing trouble the monastery, [3] but is simply content with what he finds; he should be received for however long he wants. [4] Indeed, if he reasonably and with humble charity criticizes or suggests something, the abbot should prudently consider whether the Lord may not have sent him for this very reason.

[5] If he later wishes to fix his stability there this wish should not be refused, especially since his time as a guest allowed his life to be evaluated.

Apr 16; Aug 16; Dec 16

[6] But if during that time he was found to be fussy or prone to vice, not only should he be refused membership in the community, [7] but he should also be courteously told to depart, lest others be corrupted by his misery.

[8] If, however, he is not the sort who deserves to be sent away, he should not only be received at his request into membership with the community; [9] he should, rather, be persuaded to stay so that by his example others may be taught, [10] because in every place we serve one Lord and fight under one King. [11] And if the abbot perceives that he is of this kind, he may put him in a somewhat higher place.

¹² Non solum autem monachum, sed etiam de suprascriptis gradibus sacerdotum vel clericorum stabilire potest abbas in maiori quam ingrediuntur loco, si eorum talem perspexerit esse vitam.

¹³ Caveat autem abbas ne aliquando de alio noto monasterio monachum ad habitandum suscipiat sine consensu abbatis eius aut litteras commendaticias, ¹⁴ quia scriptum est: *Quod tibi non vis fieri, alio ne feceris.*

LXII DE SACERDOTIBUS MONASTERII

¹ Si quis abbas sibi presbyterum vel diaconem ordinari petierit, de suis eligat qui dignus sit sacerdotio fungi. ² Ordinatus autem caveat elationem aut superbiam, ³ nec quicquam praesumat nisi quod ei ab abbate praecipitur, sciens se multo magis disciplinae regulari subdendum. ⁴ Nec occasione sacerdotii obliviscatur regulae oboedientiam et disciplinam, sed magis ac magis in Deum proficiat.

⁵ Locum vero illum semper attendat quod ingressus est in monasterio, ⁶ praeter officium altaris, et si forte electio congregationis et voluntas abbatis pro vitae merito eum promovere voluerint. ⁷ Qui tamen regulam decanis vel praepositis constitutam sibi servare sciat. ⁸ Quod si aliter praesumpserit, non sacerdos sed rebellio iudicetur.

¹² Not only a monk, but also one from the aforementioned grades of priests or clerics may be established by the abbot in a higher place than that of their time of entrance, if he perceives that their life merits it.

¹³ But the abbot must be careful never to receive permanently a monk from another known monastery without the consent of his abbot or letters of recommendation, ¹⁴ for it is written: *What you do not want done to yourself, do not do to another* (TOBIT 4:16).

Apr 17; Aug 17; Dec 17

CHAPTER 62: CONCERNING THE PRIESTS OF THE MONASTERY

¹ If any abbot requests to have a priest or deacon ordained for himself, he should choose from among his own one who is worthy to function as a priest. ² The one who is ordained is to cautious of arrogance and pride ³ and not presume to do anything he has not been commanded by the abbot, knowing that he will be even more subject to the discipline of the Rule. ⁴ His priesthood must not cause him to forget the obedience and discipline of the Rule; rather he should advance more and more towards God.

⁵ He is to always regard as his place that which corresponds to his entrance into the monastery, ⁶ except with regard to the service of the altar, or if the choice of the community and the will of the abbot promote him on account of the merit of his life. ⁷ Nevertheless, he is to know how to keep the rule constituted for deans and priors. ⁸ Should he presume to do otherwise he will be judged not a priest, but a rebel.

⁹ Et saepe admonitus si non correxerit, etiam episcopus adhibeatur in testimonio. ¹⁰ Quod si nec sic emendaverit, clarescentibus culpis, proiciatur de monasterio, ¹¹ si tamen talis fuerit eius contumacia ut subdi aut oboedire regulae nolit.

LXIII DE ORDINE CONGREGATIONIS

¹ Ordines suos in monasterio ita conservent ut conversationis tempus ut vitae meritum discernit utque abbas constituerit. ² Qui abbas non conturbet gregem sibi commissum nec, quasi libera utens potestate, iniuste disponat aliquid, ³ sed cogitet semper quia de omnibus iudiciis et operibus suis redditurus est Deo rationem.

⁴ Ergo secundum ordines quos constituerit vel quos habuerint ipsi fratres sic accedant ad pacem, ad communionem, ad psalmum imponendum, in choro standum; ⁵ et in omnibus omnino locis aetas non discernat ordines nec praeiudicet, ⁶ quia Samuel et Daniel pueri presbyteros iudicaverunt.

⁷ Ergo excepto hos quos, ut diximus, altiori consilio abbas praetulerit vel degradaverit certis ex causis, reliqui omnes ut convertuntur ita sint, ⁸ ut verbi gratia qui secunda hora diei venerit in monasterio iuniorem se noverit illius esse qui prima hora venit diei, cuiuslibet aetatis aut dignitatis sit, ⁹ pueris per omnia ab omnibus disciplina conservata.

[9] And if after frequent admonition he does not amend, the bishop himself is to be brought in as a witness. [10] If even then he does not amend, and his guilt is well-known, he is to be expelled from the monastery; [11] but only if his stubbornness is such that he will not submit or obey the Rule.

Apr 18; Aug 18; Dec 18

CHAPTER 63: RANK IN THE COMMUNITY

[1] They are to keep their rank in the monastery which the time of their entry and the merit of their lives determines, or as the abbot constitutes. [2] For the abbot is not to disturb the flock committed to him, nor, acting as if his power were unlimited, establish anything unjustly: [3] instead he is always to ponder that for all his judgments and deeds *he will have to give an account to God* (*cf.* LUKE 16:2).

[4] It is, therefore, in that order which he has constituted or which the brothers already have in relation to each other that they are to approach for the kiss of peace and Communion, intone psalms, and stand in choir: [5] and in absolutely every place, age is not to decide the order or be prejudicial to it; [6] for Samuel and Daniel were children when they judged the elders (I SAMUEL 3; DANIEL 13:44-62).

[7] Therefore, with the exception of those whom (as we have said) the abbot, after taking advice promotes, or demotes for certain reasons; all the rest are to have the order of their entry: [8] thus, for example, one who enters the monastery at the second hour of the day must know that he is junior to one who came at the first hour, whatever his age or dignity. [9] But children are to be kept under discipline in all matters and by everyone.

[10] Iuniores igitur priores suos honorent, priores minores suos diligant. [11] In ipsa appellatione nominum nulli liceat alium puro appellare nomine, [12] sed priores iuniores suos fratrum nomine, iuniores autem priores suos nonnos vocent, quod intellegitur paterna reverentia. [13] Abbas autem, quia vices Christi creditur agere, dominus et abbas vocetur, non sua assumptione sed honore et amore Christi; [14] ipse autem cogitet et sic se exhibeat ut dignus sit tali honore.

[15] Ubicumque autem sibi obviant fratres, iunior priorem benedictionem petat. [16] Transeunte maiore minor surgat et det ei locum sedendi, nec praesumat iunior consedere nisi ei praecipiat senior suus, [17] ut fiat quod scriptum est: *Honore invicem praevenientes.*

[18] Pueri parvi vel adulescentes in oratorio vel ad mensas cum disciplina ordines suos consequantur. [19] Foris autem vel ubiubi, et custodiam habeant et disciplinam, usque dum ad intellegibilem aetatem perveniant.

[10] The juniors, therefore, are to honor their elders, and the elders love the younger. [11] In calling each other by name, no one is to address the other by his simple name; [12] rather, the elders are to call the juniors 'brother,' and the younger call their elders *nonnus,* which means 'reverend father.' [13] But the abbot, since he is believed to represent Christ, is to be called 'Lord' and 'abbot;' not for his own sake, but out of honor and love for Christ. [14] Let him ponder this, and behave in such a way as to be worthy of such honor.

[15] Wherever the brothers meet one another the junior is to ask a blessing of the elder. [16] And when a superior passes by, the subject is to rise and give him a place to sit; nor should the junior presume to sit unless his senior bids him: [17] let it be as it is written, *outdo one another in showing honor* (ROMANS 12:10).

[18] Small children and adolescents in the oratory or at table are to keep with discipline to their proper ranks. [19] But outside or wherever else they may be, they are to receive care and discipline until they reach the age of reason.

(cf. RM 93, title)

LXIV DE ORDINANDO
ABBATE

[1] In abbatis ordinatione illa semper consideretur ratio ut hic constituatur quem sive omnis concors congregatio secundum timorem Dei, sive etiam pars quamvis parva congregationis saniore consilio elegerit. [2] Vitae autem merito et sapientiae doctrina eligatur qui ordinandus est, etiam si ultimus fuerit in ordine congregationis.

[3] Quod si etiam omnis congregatio vitiis suis—quod quidem absit—consentientem personam pari consilio elegerit, [4] et vitia ipsa aliquatenus in notitia episcopi ad cuius dioecesim pertinet locus ipse vel ad abbates aut christianos vicinos claruerint, [5] prohibeant pravorum praevalere consensum, sed domui Dei dignum constituant dispensatorem, [6] scientes pro hoc se recepturos mercedem bonam, si illud caste et zelo Dei faciant, sicut e diverso peccatum si neglegant.

(cf. RM 15:35; 27:25; 3:72)

[7] Ordinatus autem abbas cogitet semper quale onus suscepit et cui *redditurus est rationem vilicationis suae,* [8] sciatque sibi oportere prodesse magis quam praeesse.

CHAPTER 64: THE APPOINTMENT OF THE ABBOT

[1] In appointing an abbot this should always be the guiding principle: the one selected is to be chosen by the whole community acting in concord in the fear of God, or by some part of the community, however small, which possesses sounder counsel. [2] It is for the merit of his life and the wisdom of his teaching that the one appointed should be chosen, even if he comes last in community rank.

[3] But even if it were the entire community that acted together in electing a person (and may this never happen!) who consented to their vices, [4] if these vices somehow came to the notice of the bishop in whose diocese the place belongs, or if they were perceived by the neighboring abbots or Christians, [5] then they would be obliged to prevent this depraved consensus from prevailing and to constitute instead a worthy steward for the house of God, [6] knowing that for this they will receive a good reward if acting purely and out of zeal for God; and that to neglect this would on the contrary be sinful.

[7] The one appointed abbot should always ponder what a burden he has received, and to whom *he will have to give an account of his stewardship* (LUKE 16:2) [8] and he must know how much more fitting it is to provide for others than to preside over them.

[9] Oportet **ergo eum** esse **doctum** lege **divina, ut sciat et** sit unde *proferat nova et vetera,* castum, sobrium, misericordem,[10]et semper *superexaltet misericordiam iudicio,* ut idem *ipse consequatur.*

[11] **Oderit vitia, diligat fratres.** [12] **In ipsa autem correptione prudenter agat et** ne quid nimis, **ne dum nimis eradere cupit aeruginem frangatur vas;** [13] **suamque fragilitatem semper suspectus sit, memineritque** *calamum quassatum non conterendum.* [14] **In quibus non dicimus ut permittat nutriri vitia, sed prudenter et cum caritate ea amputet, ut viderit cuique expedire sicut iam diximus,** [15] **et studeat plus amari quam timeri.**

[16] **Non sit turbulentus et anxius, non sit nimius et obstinatus, non sit** zelotypus **et nimis suspiciosus, quia numquam requiescit;** [17] **in ipsis imperiis suis providus et consideratus, et sive secundum Deum sive secundum saeculum sit opera quam iniungit, discernat et temperet,** [18] **cogitans discretionem sancti Iacob dicentis:** *Si greges meos plus in ambulando fecero laborare, morientur cuncti una die.* [19] **Haec ergo aliaque testimonia discretionis matris virtutum sumens, sic omnia temperet ut sit et fortes quod cupiant et infirmi non refugiant.**

[9] He should **therefore** be **learned in divine** law, so that he knows how to *bring forth new things and old* (MATTHEW 13:52); he is to be chaste, sober, merciful, [10] and he should always *allow mercy to triumph above judgment* (JAMES 2:13), so that *he may receive mercy* (MATTHEW 5:7).

[11] He is to hate vices and love the brothers. [12] But in correcting them he is to act prudently and avoid extremes, lest in trying too ardently to scrape off the rust, he breaks the vessel: [13] his own frailty he must always keep before his eyes, recalling that *the bruised reed is not to be broken* (ISAIAH 42:3). [14] By this we do not mean he should permit vices to sprout: on the contrary, he should prudently and charitably cut them off as he sees best for each, as we have said: [15] and he should strive to be loved rather than feared.

[16] He is not to be turbulent and anxious, nor excessive and obstinate, nor jealous and prone to suspicion; for otherwise he will never be at rest: [17] In his commands he is to be farsighted and considerate; and whether the works he enjoins concern God or the world he is to be discerning and moderate, [18] reflecting on the discretion of holy Jacob, who said: *If I drive my flocks too hard, they will all die in one day* (GENESIS 33:13). [19] Thus by means of this and other examples of discretion, the mother of virtue, he is to regulate everything so that the strong have something to yearn for and the weak are not frightened away.

[20] Et praecipue ut praesentem regulam in omnibus conservet, [21] ut dum bene ministraverit audiat a Domino quod servus bonus qui erogavit triticum conservis suis in tempore suo: [22] *Amen dico vobis,* ait, *super omnia bona sua constituit eum.*

(cf. RM 92: 2.37; 93:47-66)

LXV DE PRAEPOSITO MONASTERII

[1] Saepius quidem contigit ut per ordinationem praepositi scandala gravia in monasteriis oriantur, [2] dum sint aliqui maligno spiritu superbiae inflati et aestimantes se secundos esse abbates, assumentes sibi tyrannidem, scandala nutriunt et dissensiones in congregationes faciunt, [3] et maxime in illis locis ubi ab eodem sacerdote vel ab eis abbatibus qui abbatem ordinant, ab ipsis etiam et praepositus ordinatur. [4] Quod quam sit absurdum facile advertitur, quia ab ipso initio ordinationis materia ei datur superbiendi, [5] dum ei suggeritur a cogitationibus suis exutum eum esse a potestate abbatis sui, [6] quia ab ipsis es et tu ordinatus a quibus et abbas.

[7] Hinc suscitantur invidiae, rixae, detractiones, aemulationes, dissensiones, exordinationes, [8] ut dum contraria sibi abbas praepositusque sentiunt, et ipsorum necesse est sub hanc dissensionem animas periclitari, [9] et hi qui sub ipsis sunt, dum adulantur partibus, eunt in perditionem. [10] Cuius periculi malum illos respicit in capite qui talius inordinationis se fecerunt auctores.

20 And in particular he is to keep this Rule in every way, 21 so that, having ministered well, he will hear from the Lord what was heard by the good servant who gave grain to his fellow-servants in due season: 22 *Truly I say to you*, he said, *he sets him over all his goods* (MATTHEW 24:27).

Apr 22; Aug 22; Dec 22

CHAPTER 65: THE PRIOR OF THE MONASTERY

1 Very often it happens that through the appointment of a prior grave scandals arise in monasteries; 2 for there are some who, inflated by a malignant spirit of pride and esteeming themselves to be second abbots, assume for themselves tyrannical power, and so feed scandals and create dissensions in the community: 3 and this occurs especially in those places where it is by the same bishop or the same abbots who ordain the abbot that the prior is himself ordained. 4 How absurd this is may easily be seen: for as soon as he is ordained he is given an incentive to pride, 5 his thoughts suggesting to him that he is free from the authority of his abbot 6 since he has been ordained by the very same persons.

7 Thus arise jealousies, quarrels, detractions, competitiveness, dissensions, and depositions from office. 8 And while the abbot and prior are opposed to one another it necessarily follows that through this dissension their souls are endangered: 9 and those who are subject to them, being flattered as followers, go to their destruction. 10 The blame for this perilous evil rests on the head of those who were the authors of such disorders.

(RM 93:74-88)

[11] Ideo nos vidimus expedire propter pacis caritatisque custodiam in abbatis pendere arbitrio ordinationem monasterii sui; [12] et si potest fieri per decanos ordinetur, ut ante disposuimus, omnis utilitas monasterii, prout abbas disposuerit, [13] ut, dum pluribus committitur, unus non superbiat.

[14] Quod si aut locus expetit aut congregatio petierit rationabiliter cum humilitate e abbas iudicaverit expedire, [15] quemcumque elegerit abbas cum consilio fratrum timentium Deum ordinet ipse sibi praepositum

[16] Qui tamen praepositus illa agat cum reverentia quae ab abbate suo ei iniuncta fuerint, nihil contra abbatis voluntatem aut ordinationem faciens, [17] quia quantum praelatus est ceteris, ita eum oportet sollicitius observare praecepta regulae.

[18] Qui praepositus si repertus fuerit vitiosus aut elatione deceptus superbire, aut contemptor sanctae regulae fuerit comprobatus, admoneatur verbis usque quater, [19] si non emendaverit, adhibeatur ei correptio disciplinae regularis. [20] Quod si neque sic correxerit, tunc deiciatur de ordine praepositurae et alius qui dignus est in loco eius surrogetur. [21] Quod si et postea in congregatione quietus et oboediens non fuerit, etiam de monasterio pellatur. [22] Cogitet tamen abbas se de omnibus iudiciis suis Deo *reddere rationem* ne forte invidiae aut zeli flamma urat animam.

11 Therefore we regard it expedient for the preservation of peace and charity that the organization of his monastery depend on the will of the abbot: 12 and, if possible, deans should conduct (as we have already arranged) all the affairs of the monastery according to the disposition of the abbot; 13 so that, what is committed to several will not cause pride in any single one.

14 But if either the locale requires it or the community reasonably and with humility requests it, and if the abbot judges it expedient, 15 the abbot (with the counsel of God-fearing brothers) is to choose whomever he wishes and himself ordain him prior.

16 But this prior is to perform with reverence what the abbot demands of him, doing nothing contrary to the abbot's will or organization; 17 for the more he is elevated above the rest, the more solicitously he ought to observe the precepts of the Rule.

18 If this prior proves to have vices, or is deceived by the haughtiness of pride, or proves to have contempt for the holy Rule, he is to be verbally admonished up to four times; 19 if he does not amend, the discipline of the Rule is to be applied to him. 20 But if even then he does not amend, he is to be deposed from the office of prior and another who is worthy be substituted in his place. 21 But if afterwards he is not quiet and obedient in the community, he is to be expelled from the monastery. 22 Nevertheless, the abbot is to bear in mind that he must *give an account* to God of all his judgments, lest the flame of envy or jealousy be kindled in his soul.

(RM 95:1-3, 17-21; 24: 15-17, 26-33)

LXVI DE OSTIARIIS MONASTERII

[1] Ad portam monasterii ponatur senex sapiens, qui sciat accipere reponsum et reddere, et cuius maturitas eum non sinat vagari. [2] Qui portarius cellam debebit habere iuxta portam, ut venientes semper praesentem inveniant a quo responsum accipiant. [3] Et mox ut aliquis pulsaverit aut pauper clamaverit, Deo gratias respondeat aut Benedic, [4] et cum omni mansuetudine timoris Dei reddat responsum festinanter cum fervore caritatis. [5] Qui portarius si indiget solacio iuniorem fratrem accipiat.

[6] Monasterium autem, si possit fieri, ita debet constitui ut omnia necessaria, id est aqua, molendinum, hortum, vel artes diversas intra monasterium exerceantur, [7] ut non sit necessitas monachis vagandi foris, quia omnino non expedit animabus eorum.

[8] Hanc autem regulam saepius volumus in congregatione legi, ne quis fratrum se de ignorantia excuset.

CHAPTER 66: **THE MONASTERY PORTERS**

[1] At the door of the monastery there should be placed a wise old man who knows how to take a message and give one, and whose maturity keeps him from wandering. [2] This porter ought to have his room near the door, so that those who arrive will always find someone present to take their message. [3] As soon as anyone knocks or a poor person calls out he should respond, *Thanks be to God,* or *Please give your blessing;* [4] and with all the gentleness of the fear of God, he is to respond quickly with the fervor of love. [5] If the porter requires help a younger brother should be given to him.

[6] As regards the monastery: if possible it is to be so constituted that all necessities, such as water, mill, garden, and various crafts may be practiced within the monastery [7] so there will be no necessity for the monks to wander outside; for this is not at all good for their souls.

[8] As regards this Rule: we wish it to be frequently read in the community, so that none of the brothers may excuse themselves on account of ignorance.

(RM 66:1-7; 20:4)

LXVII DE FRATRIBUS IN VIAM DIRECTIS

[1] Dirigendi fratres in via **omnium fratrum vel abbatis se orationi commendent,** [2] **et semper ad** orationem **ultimam operis Dei commemoratio omnium** absentum fiat. [3] Revertentes **autem de via fratres ipso die quo redeunt per omnes canonicas horas,** dum expletur opus Dei, prostrati solo oratorii [4] ab omnibus petant orationem propter excessos, ne qui forte surripuerint in via visus aut auditus malae rei aut otiosi sermonis.

[5] Nec praesumat quisquam referre alio quaecumque foris monasterium viderit aut audierit, quia plurima destructio est. [6] Quod si quis praesumpserit, vindictae regulari subiaceat. [7] Similiter et qui praesumpserit claustra monasterii egredi vel quocumque ire vel quippiam quamvis parvum sine iussione abbatis facere.

LXVIII SI FRATRI IMPOSSIBILIA INIUNGANTUR

[1] Si cui fratri aliqua forte gravia aut impossibilia iniunguntur, suscipiat quidem iubentis imperium cum omni mansuetudine et oboedientia. [2] Quod si omnino virium suarum mensuram viderit pondus oneris excedere, impossibilitatis suae causas ei qui sibi praeest patienter et opportune suggerat, [3] non superbiendo aut resistendo vel contradicendo. [4] Quod si post suggestionem suam in sua sententia prioris imperium perduraverit, sciat iunior ita sibi expedire, [5] et ex caritate, confidens de adiutorio Dei, oboediat.

CHAPTER 67: **BROTHERS SENT ON A JOURNEY**

[1] Brothers sent on a journey **are to commend themselves to the prayers of all the brothers and of the abbot;** [2] **and always, at the last** prayer **of the Work of God, all those who are** absent **should be remembered.**
[3] **Brothers** returning **from a journey, on the same day they come back, are to lie prostrate on the floor of the oratory at all the canonical** hours at the end **of the Work of God:** [4] **they** request the prayers **of all for their faults, in case they have seen or heard anything evil on their journey or have fallen into idle talk.**
[5] **No one shall presume to tell others what he may have seen or heard outside the monastery, for this is very destructive.** [6] **If anyone so presumes, he is to be subjected to the punishment of the Rule.** [7] **It is to be the same with one who presumes to leave the enclosure of the monastery, whether to go anywhere or do anything, however small, without the order of the abbot.**

CHAPTER 68: **IF IMPOSSIBLE THINGS ARE COMMANDED OF A BROTHER**

[1] **If a brother is commanded to do hard or impossible things, he should receive the order of his superior with all gentleness and obedience.** [2] **But if he sees that the measure of his strength is exceeded by the weight of the burden, he is to explain the cause of his incapacity to his superior patiently and at an opportune time,** [3] **without showing pride, resistance, or contradiction.** [4] **But if after his explanation the superior persists in his command, the junior must know that this is best for him;** [5] **and out of love, confident of God's help, he is to obey.**

161

LXIX   UT IN MONASTERIO NON PRAESUMAT ALTER ALTERUM DEFENDERE

[1] Praecavendum est ne quavis occasione praesumat alter alium defendere monachum in monasterio aut quasi tueri, [2] etiam si qualivis consanguinitatis propinquitate iungantur. [3] Nec quolibet modo id a monachis praesumatur, quia exinde gravissima occasio scandalorum oriri potest. [4] Quod si quis haec transgressus fuerit, acrius coerceatur.

(*cf.* RM 14:79)

LXX   UT NON PRAESUMAT PASSIM ALIQUIS CAEDERE

[1] Vitetur in monasterio omnis praesumptionis occasio; [2] atque constituimus ut nulli liceat quemquam fratrum suorum excommunicare aut caedere, nisi cui potestas ab abbate data fuerit. [3] Peccantes autem coram omnibus arguantur ut ceteri metum habeant. [4] Infantum vero usque quindecim annorum aetates disciplinae diligentia ab omnibus et custodia sit; [5] sed et hoc cum omni mensura et ratione.

[6] Nam in fortiori aetate qui praesumit aliquatenus sine praecepto abbatis vel in ipsis infantibus sine discretione exarserit, disciplinae regulari subiaceat, [7] quia scriptum est: Quod tibi non vis fieri, alio ne feceris.

Apr 27; Aug 27; Dec 27

CHAPTER 69: IN THE MONASTERY ONE MAY NOT PRESUME TO DEFEND ANOTHER

[1] Every precaution must be taken that no one in the monastery presumes on any occasion to defend another monk or to act as his protector, [2] even if they are closely related by some sort of blood ties. [3] The monks must not presume to do this in any way whatever, because from it may arise the most grievous occasions of scandals. [4] If anyone transgresses this, he is to be severely punished.

Apr 28; Aug 28; Dec 28

CHAPTER 70: THAT THEY MAY NOT PRESUME TO STRIKE ONE ANOTHER AT WILL

[1] So as to avoid in the monastery every occasion of presumption, [2] we decree that no one has the right to excommunicate or strike any of his brothers, unless he has received power do to so by the abbot. [3] *For sinners are to be reproved before all, so that the rest may have fear* (I TIMOTHY 5:20). [4] Children, however, up to fifteen years of age are to be kept under diligent and watchful discipline by all: [5] yet this too is to be done reasonably and with all measure.

[6] For if anyone without precept from the abbot presumes authority over those who are above that age, or if he acts towards children without discretion, he is to be subjected to the discipline of the Rule; [7] for it is written: *What you do not wish done to you, do not do to another* (TOBIT 4:16).

163

LXXI UT OBOEDIENTES SIBI SINT INVICEM

[1] Oboedientiae bonum non solum abbati exhibendum est ab omnibus, sed etiam sibi invicem ita oboediant fratres, [2] scientes per hanc oboedientiae viam se ituros ad Deum. [3] Praemisso ergo abbatis aut praepositorum qui ab eo constituuntur imperio, cui non permittimus privata imperia praeponi, [4] de cetero omnes iuniores prioribus suis omni caritate et sollicitudine oboediant. [5] Quod si quis contentiosus reperitur, corripiatur.

[6] Si quis autem frater pro quavis minima causa ab abbate vel a quocumque priore suo corripitur quolibet modo, [7] vel si leviter senserit animos prioris cuiuscumque contra se iratos vel commotos quamvis modice, [8] mox sine mora tamdiu prostratus in terra ante pedes eius iaceat satisfaciens, usque dum benedictione sanetur illa commotio. [9] Quod qui contempserit facere, aut corporali vindictae subiaceat aut, si contumax fuerit, de monasterio expellatur.

Apr 29; Aug 29; Dec 29

CHAPTER 71: THAT THEY SHOULD OBEY ONE ANOTHER

[1] Not only is the blessing of obedience to be shown by all to the abbot; the brothers must also obey one another, [2] knowing that by this path of obedience they go to God. [3] The commands, therefore, of the abbot or the superiors appointed by him (to which we allow no unofficial orders to be preferred) are to be given precedence. [4] For the rest let all the younger brothers obey their elders with all love and courtesy. [5] Anyone who is found to be quarrelsome is to be corrected.

[6] If anyone is rebuked by the abbot or by any superior in any way for however small a cause, [7] or if he comes to believe that any superior is angered or perplexed about him, however trivially; [8] he should immediately and without delay cast himself on the ground at his feet, remaining there to do penance until the turmoil is healed by the other's blessing. [9] But if any one is too haughty to do this, he should be subjected to corporal punishment: if he remains unyielding, he must be expelled from the monastery.

LXXII   DE ZELO BONO QUOD DEBENT MONACHI HABERE

[1] Sicut est zelus amaritudinis malus qui separat a Deo et ducit ad infernum, [2] ita est zelus bonus qui separat a vitia, et ducit ad Deum et ad vitam aeternam. [3] Hunc ergo zelum ferventissimo amore exerceant monachi, [4] id est *ut honore se invicem praeveniant.*

[5] Infirmitates suas sive corporum sive morum patientissime tolerent; [6] obedientiam sibi certatim impendant; [7] nullus quod sibi utile judicat sequatur, sed quod magis alio; [8] caritatem fraternitatis casto impendant; [9] amore Deum timeant; [10] abbatem suum sincera et humili caritate diligant; [11] Christo omnino nihil praeponant, [12] qui nos pariter ad vitam aeternam perducat. Amen.

CHAPTER 72: THE GOOD ZEAL THAT MONKS OUGHT TO HAVE

[1] Just as there is an evil zeal of bitterness which separates from God and leads to hell, [2] so there is a good zeal which separates from vices and leads to God and to life everlasting. [3] This zeal then, should be practiced by monks with the most fervent love. [4] That is: *they should outdo one another in showing honor.* (ROMANS 12:10)

[5] Let them most patiently endure one another's infirmities, whether of body or of character. [6] Let them compete in showing obedience to one another. [7] None should follow what he judges useful for himself, but rather what is better for another: [8] They should practice fraternal charity with a pure love; [9] to God offering loving reverence, [10] loving their abbot with sincere and humble affection, [11] preferring nothing whatever to Christ, [12] and may he bring us all together to life everlasting. Amen.

LXXIII DE HOC QUOD NON OMNIS IUSTITIAE OBSERVATIO IN HAC SIT REGULA CONSTITUTA

[1] Regulam autem hanc descripsimus, ut hanc observantes in monasteriis aliquatenus vel honestatem morum aut initium conversationis nos demonstremus habere. [2] Ceterum ad perfectionem conversationis qui festinat, sunt doctrinae sanctorum patrum, quarum observatio perducat hominem ad celsitudinem perfectionis. [3] Quae enim pagina aut qui sermo divinae auctoritatis veteris ac novi testamenti non est rectissima norma vita humanae?

[4] Aut quis liber sanctorum catholicorum patrum hoc non resonat ut recto cursu perveniamus ad creatorem nostrum? [5] Necnon et Collationes Patrum et Instituta et Vitas eorum, sed et Regula sancti patris nostri Basilii, [6] quid aliud sunt nisi bene viventium et oboedientium monachorum instrumenta virtutum. [7] Nobis autem desidiosis et male viventibus atque neglegentibus rubor confusionis est.

[8] Quisquis ergo ad patriam caelestem festinas, hanc minimam inchoationis regulam descriptam, adiuvante Christo, perfice, [9] et tunc demum ad maiora quae supra commemoravimus doctrinae virtutumque culmina, Deo protegente, pervenies. Amen.

May 1; Aug 31; Dec 31

CHAPTER 73: THE WHOLE OF JUST OBSERVANCE IS NOT CONTAINED IN THIS RULE

[1] We have written this Rule so that, by observing it in monasteries, we may demonstrate that we have somewhat grasped honorable behavior and the beginnings of ascetical practice. [2] But for those hastening to the perfection of ascetical practice there are the teachings of the Holy Fathers, the observance of which leads one to the heights of perfection. [3] For what page or what words are there in the divinely–inspired Old and New Testaments that are not a most direct norm for human life?

[4] Or what book of the Holy Catholic Fathers does not resoundingly proclaim the direct path by which we may reach our Creator? [5] Moreover, the *Conferences* of the Fathers, their *Institutes* and their *Lives*, as well as the Rule of our holy Father Basil— [6] what else are these for good–living and obedient monks other than instruments of virtue? [7] But to us who are lazy, bad–living, and negligent they bring the blush of shame.

[8] Whoever you are, therefore, hastening toward your heavenly homeland; fulfill with the help of Christ this little Rule for beginners we have written: [9] and then at last you will arrive under God's protection at the loftier summits of doctrine and virtue we have spoken of above. Amen.

INDEX

abbas *(abbot)* 1.2; 2.title; 2.1, 3, 4 ,6, 7, 11, 19, 23, 30; 3.1,
5, 9, 11; 4.61; 5.12; 7.44; 9.5; 11.6, 7, 8, 9, 10; 21.2, 3;
22.2; 24.2; 25.5; 26.1; 27.title; 1, 5; 28.2, 6; 31.4, 12, 15;
32.1, 3; 33.2, 5; 36.6, 10; 39.6; 41.4; 42.10; 43.5, 11; 44.3,
4, 5, 6, 8, 9; 46.3, 5; 47.1, 2, 4; 48.25; 49.8, 10; 50.2; 51.2;
53.12, 13, 16; 54.1, 2, 3; 55.3, 8, 16, 17, 18, 20, 21;
56.title, 1; 57.1, 3; 58.19, 29; 60.4; 61.4, 11, 12, 13; 62.1,
3, 6; 63.1, 2, 7, 13; 64.title, 1, 4, 7; 65.2, 3, 5, 6, 8, 11, 12,
14, 15, 16, 22; 67.1, 7; 70.2, 6; 71.1, 3, 6; 72.10

abbot - abbas

to abstain - abstinere

abstinentia *(abstinence)* 49.4; 49.5

abstinere *(to abstain)* 36.9; 39.11; 40.4; 49.4

accipere *(to receive)* Prol. 27; 2.3; 5.18; 22.2; 24.5; 33.2;
34.title; 35.12,17,18; 38.4.10; 43.19; 48.15; 54.1;
55.9,12,13,14,17; 66.1,2,5.

actus *(action/deed/performance)* Prol. 5, 21, 22; 2.8,17;
4.20,48; 7.6;

adimplere *(to fulfill)* 4.63,76; 7.42;

adiutorium *(help/assistance)* Prol. 41; 17.3; 18.1; 35.17; 68.5

adiuvare *(to help)* 1.13; 18.1; 31.17; 35.16, 17; 73.8

admonere *(to admonish)* Prol. 9; 2.25; 23.2; 33.7; 40.9; 65.18

admonitio *(admonition)* Prol. 1; 2.27; 62.9

aedificare *(to edify/build)* Prol. 33; 38.12; 42.3; 47.3; 53.9

aedificatio *(edification)* 6.3; 38.9

aestimare *(to estimate)* 7.13; 38, 64; 65.2

aeternus *(eternal)* 4.46; 5.3, 10; 6.8; 7.11; 72.2, 12

alleluia 9.9; 11.6; 12.2; 15.title,1,3,4

altare *(altar)* 31.10; 58.20,29; 59.2; 62.6; 63.7

amare *(to love)* 2.17; 4.13, 52, 54, 64, 68; 7.31; 64.15

to amend - emendare

amor *(love)* 4.21, 72; 5.10; 7.34, 69; 63.13; 72.3, 9

amputare *(to amputate)* 2.26; 33.1; 55.11, 18; 64.14

angustus *(narrow)* Prol. 48; 5.11

anima *(soul)* 2.29, 31, 33, 34, 37, 38; 4.1; 7.4, 9; 27.6; 31.8;
41.5; 46.5; 48.1; 53.21; 57.6; 58.6; 65.8, 22; 66.7

antiphon - antiphona

antiphona 9.3,4; 11.4; 12.1; 13.2; 14.2; 15.3; 17.6,7,9; 24.4;
45.1; 47.2

ardent desire - concupiscentia
to ardently desire - concupiscere
to arise - surgere
ars *(art/craft)* 4.75; 46.1; 48.24; 57.1, 2, 3; 66.6
artifex *(craftsman)* 57.title,1,4
ascendere *(to ascend/climb)* 7.5; 7.6; 7.7; 7.9; 7.67
to assign - assignare
to assign - deputare
assignare *(to assign)* 32.3; 42.7; 53.21
auctoritas *(authority)* 9.8; 37.1; 73.3
auris *(ear)* Prol. 1, 9, 11, 18; 4.77; 5.5
avaritia *(avarice)* 31.12; 57.7

to become proud - superbire
to believe - credere
benedicere *(to bless)* 4.32; 7.43; 9.5; 25.6; 35.16; 40.8;
44.10; 60.4; 66.3
benedictio *(blessing, benediction)* 11.10; 12.4; 17.10;
35.17, 18; 38.4; 53.24; 63.15; 71.8
bodily - corporalis
body - corpus
book - codex
to bow - incumbere

caelestis: *(heavenly)* 7.5; 73.8
caelum *(heaven)* 7.8, 13, 27, 65
to call - vocare
canere *(to sing)* 9.9; 17.title; 18.12
cantare *(to sing/intone)* 9.5, 6; 11.3; 38.12; 47.3
care/charge - cura
caritas *(charity/love)* Prol. 47; 2.22; 4.26; 7.67; 27.4; 35.6;
53.3; 61.4; 64.14; 65.11; 66.4; 68.5; 71.4; 72.8, 10
caro *(flesh)* 1.5; 4.59; 7.12, 23; 25.4; 36.9; 39.11
castitas *(chastity)* 4.64
castus *(chaste)* 64.6, 9
catholicus *(catholic)* 9.8; 73.4
cella *(cell)* 1.10; 22.4; 36.7; 53.21; 58.4, 5, 11; 66.2
change - emendatio
charity/love - caritas
chaste - castus

chastity - castitas

to choose - eligere

chorus *(choir)* 43.4,11; 44.5; 63.4

christianus *(Christian)* 39.8; 64.4

Christus *(Christ)* Prol. 3, 28, 50; 2.2, 20; 4.10, 21, 50, 72; 5.2; 7.69; 36.1; 53.1, 7, 15; 63.13; 72.11; 73.8

cibus *(food/meal)* 24.5; 25.5, 6; 39.title; 43.17, 18; 49.5, 7.

claustrum/clausura *(cloister/enclosure)* 4.78; 6.8; 67.7

clericus *(cleric)* 60.8; 61.12

cloister/enclosure - claustrum/clausura

codex *(book)* 9.5, 8; 10.2; 11.2; 33.3; 38.1; 48.15, 16

cogitare *(to reflect/ponder)* 2.34; 55.22; 63.3, 14; 64.7, 18; 65.22

cogitatio *(thought)* 1.5; 4.50; 7.12, 14, 15, 16, 17, 18, 44; 65.5

collatio *(conference)* 42.3, 5; 73.5

colloqui *(converse)* 25.2; 53.23, 24

to come - venire

to command - iubere

commandment - mandatum

common - communis

communio *(communion)* 38.2, 10; 63.4

communis *(common)* 5.9; 7.55; 33.6; 43.15

community - congregatio

compunctio *(compunction)* 20.3; 49.4

concupiscentia *(ardent desire)* 4.46; 7.25

concupiscere *(to ardently desire)* 4.6

conference - collatio

congregatio *(community)* 3.1; 4.78; 17.6; 21.1; 31.1, 2, 17; 35.4,5; 46.3; 53.13; 58.14, 22, 23; 61.8; 62.6; 63.title; 64.1, 2, 3; 65.2, 14, 21; 66.8

conservare *(to keep)* 58.27; 63.1, 9; 64.20

considerare *(to consider)* 19.6; 36.4; 37.2; 40.5; 48.25; 55.20, 21; 64.1; 64.17

consideratio *(consideration)* 8.1; 34.2; 37.3; 53.19; 55.3

consilium *(council/counsel)* 3.title, 2, 3, 4, 12, 13; 63.7; 64.1, 3; 65.15

consolari *(to console)* 4.19; 27.3; 35.16

consolatio *(support)* 1.5

contrarius *(contrary)* 2.13; 7.35, 38; 23.1; 39.8; 65.8

contristare *(to sadden)* Prol. 5; 31.6, 7, 19; 34.3; 36.4; 48.7; 54.4

conversatio *(way of life)* Prol. 49; 1.3, 12; 21.1; 22.2; 58.1; 63.1; 73.1, 2

converse - colloqui

cor *(heart)* Prol. 1, 10, 26, 28, 40, 49; 2.9, 12; 3.8; 4.1, 24, 28, 50; 5.17, 18; 7.3, 8, 14, 18, 37, 44, 48, 51, 62, 65; 9.10; 12.4; 20.3; 39.9; 49.4; 52.4

corporalis *(bodily)* 23.5; 71.9

corpus *(body)* Prol. 40, 43; 2.28; 4.11; 7.9, 62; 33.4; 49.7; 53.7; 57.5; 58.25; 61.6; 72.5

to correct - corrigere/corripere

correction - correptio

correptio *(correction)* 33.8; 48.20; 64.12; 65.19

corrigere *(to correct)* 2.28; 23.4; 28.2; 45.2; 62.9; 65.20

corripere *(to correct)* 2.25, 27; 28.title; 28.1; 30.title; 32.4; 43.14; 48.19; 71.5, 6

council - consilium

cowl - cuculla

craftsman - artifex

crapula *(overindulgence)* 39.7,8,9

credere *(to believe)* 2.2, 39; 7.23, 51; 19.1, 2; 27.5; 39.1; 40.3; 48.2; 55.4; 63.13

cuculla *(cowl)* 55.4, 5, 10, 14, 19

culpa *(fault)* 2.7; 23.title; 24.1, 2; 24.3; 25.title, 1; 28.1; 44.1, 9; 45.3; 62.10

cura *(care/charge)* 2.8, 10, 38; 27.1, 6; 31.3, 9, 15; 36.1, 6, 10; 47.1; 53.15

currere *(to run)* Prol. 13, 22, 44, 49; 27.5; 43.1

custodia *(custody)* 6.1; 63.19; 65.11; 70.4

custodire *(to keep custody)* 4.48, 51; 6.1; 7.12, 68; 31.5, 8; 32.2; 49.2; 58.14

dean - decanus

death - mors

debilis *(weak/injured)* 27.7; 36.9; 39.11

decanus *(dean)* 21.title, 1, 3, 5; 62.7; 65.12

defend - defendere

defendere *(defend)* 3.4; 28.2; 69.title, 1

deificus *(deifying)* Prol. 9

deifying - deificus

delectare *(to delight in)* 7.31; 33.7

delectatio *(delight)* 7.24; 7.69

deputare *(to assign)* 7.28; 36.7; 48.17, 22; 49.9; 58.6;

desiderare *(to desire)* 4.46; 5.12; 43.19

desiderium *(a desire)* 1.8; 4.59; 5.12; 7.12, 23, 24, 31; 49.7; 60.8

Deus *(God)* Prol. 16, 31, 37, 49; 1.5, 7; 2.6, 14, 20, 35; 3.11; 4.1, 41, 42, 49, 57, 63, 74, 77; 5.9, 14, 15, 16, 18; 7.10, 11, 13, 14, 20, 23, 27, 29, 34, 40, 63, 67; 11.8, 13; 17.3; 18.1; 20.2; 21.2; 22.6, 8; 27.7; 31.2, 19; 34.3; 35.16; 35.17; 36.4, 7; 38.2; 40.1, 4, 8; 43.title, 3, 6, 10; 44.1, 7; 47.title, 1; 49.6; 50.3; 52.2, 5; 53.14, 21, 22; 55.22; 57.9; 58.2, 7; 58.8, 18; 59.1; 62.4; 63.3; 64.1, 5, 6; 64.17; 65.15, 22; 66.3, 4; 67.2, 3; 68.5; 71.2; 72.1, 2, 9; 73.9

devil - diabolus/diabolicus

devotio *(devotion)* 18.24; 20.2

diabolus/diabolicus *(devil)* Prol. 28; I.4; 53.5; 54.4; 58.28

dignus *(worthy)* 2.1; 7.65; 11.13; 21.6; 49.4; 62.1; 63.14; 64.5; 65.20

dilatare *(to open wide)* Prol. 49

dilectio *(love)* Prol. 49

diligence - diligentia

diligens *(diligent)* 4.78; 36.7

diligentia *(diligence)* 2.8; 70.4

diligere *(to love)* 4.1, 31, 71, 77; 5.16; 7.39; 63.10; 64.11; 72.10

disciple - discipulus

disciplina *(discipline)* 2.14, 22; 3.10; 7.9; 19.title; 24.1; 32.5; 34.7; 54.5; 55.17; 56.3; 58.title; 60.2, 5; 62.3, 4; 63.9, 18, 19; 65.19; 70.4, 6

discipulus *(disciple)* 2.5, 6, 11, 12, 13; 3.6; 5.9, 16, 17; 6.3, 6, 8; 36.10

discretio *(discretion)* 64.18, 19; 70.6

divinus *(divine)* Prol. 9; 2.5, 12; 7.1, 9, 39; 8.title; 9.8; 16.title; 19.1, 2; 20.4; 28.3; 31.16; 43.1; 48.1; 50.3; 53.9; 64.9; 73.3;

docere *(to teach)* Prol.12; 1.4; 2.4, 13; 6.6; 7.21; 64.9

doctrina *(teaching, doctrine)* Prol. 50; 2.5, 6, 11, 23; 21.4; 64.2; 73.2, 9

dormire *(to sleep)* 22.title, 1, 3, 5; 43.8; 58.5

dulcis *(sweet)* Prol.19; 5.14

durus *(hard)* 2.25, 28; 7.35; 58.8

to dwell - habitare

ear - auris
Easter - Pascha - - pastor
edification - aedificatio
to edify/build - aedificare
eligere *(to choose)* 1.9; 21.1, 3, 4; 31.1; 62.1; 64.1, 2, 3; 65.15
emendare *(to amend)* 2.40; 4.58; 5.19; 21.5; 23.3; 28.title, 1; 32.5; 33.8; 43.7, 9, 15; 48.20; 62.10; 65.19
emendatio *(change)* Prol.36, 47; 2.40; 29.1; 43.16, 19; 46.4
envy - invidia
to estimate - aestimare
eternal - aeternus
excommunicare *(to excommunicate)* 26.title, 1; 27.title; 28.1; 44.title, 1, 9; 51.3; 70.2
excommunicatio *(excommunication)* 23.title, 4; 24.title, 1; 26.2; 28.3; 30.2
eye - oculus

faith - fides
faithful - fidelis
to fast - ieiunare
fasting - ieiunium
father - pater
fault - culpa
to fear - timere
fear/awe - timor
fervor *(fervor)* 1.3; 41.4; 72.3
fidelis *(faithful)* 7.38
fides *(faith)* Prol.21, 49; 1.7; 53.2
fight - militare
filius *(son)* Prol.1, 5, 6, 12; 2.3, 29; 7.27; 59.title,1,8
flesh - caro
flock - grex
food - cibus
to fulfill - adimplere

given to murmuring - murmuriosus

gloria *(glory)* Prol.7, 30; 5.3; 9.2, 6; 13.9; 17.2; 18.1; 43.4, 10; 49.9; 58.22

gloriari *(to give glory)* Prol.32

glorificare *(to glorify)* 57.9

to glorify - glorificare

God - Deus

grace - gratia

gratia *(grace)* Prol.31, 41; 5.19; 20.4; 34.3; 66.3

gravis *(grave)* Prol. 46; 25.title, 1; 35.1, 13; 38.10; 42.9; 44.1; 55.17; 65.1; 68.1; 69.3

gravitas *(gravity)* 6.3; 7.60; 22.6; 42.11; 43.2; 47.4

grex *(flock)* 2.8, 32; 27.9; 28.8; 63.2; 64.18

guest - hospes

habitare *(to dwell)* Prol.22, 23, 39; 40.8; 55.1; 60.title; 61.1, 13

hard - durus

heart - cor

heaven - caelum

heavenly - caelestis

to help - adiuvare

help/assistance - adiutorium

holy - sanctus

honor 9.7; 11.9; 36.4; 53.2, 15; 63.13, 14, 17; 72.4

honorare *(to honor)* 4.8; 63.10

to hope - sperare

hope - spes

hospes *(guest)* 31.9; 42.10; 53.title, 1, 3, 6, 8, 9, 10, 12, 13, 16, 21, 23, 24; 56.1, 2; 58.4; 61.1

humble - humilis

humiliare *(to humiliate)* 6.1; 7.1, 8, 52, 53, 54, 66; 34.4; 45.1; 57.3

to humiliate - humiliare

humilis *(humble)* 2.21; 7.4, 44, 60; 53.24; 72.10

humilitas *(humility)* 3.4; 5.1; 6.7; 7.title, 5, 7, 9, 10, 31, 34, 35, 44, 49, 51, 55, 56, 59, 60, 62, 67; 20.1, 2; 27.3; 29.2; 31.7, 13; 45.2; 47.4; 53.6; 57.1; 60.5; 61.4; 65.14

ieiunare *(to fast)* 41.2

ieiunium *(fasting)* 4.13; 30.3; 38.10; 42.2, 5; 53.10, 11

incumbere *(to bow)* 2.7; 4.56; 5.10

infirm - infirmus

infirmitas *(infirmity)* 27.9; 34.2, 4; 39.1; 55.21; 72.5

infirmity - infirmitas

infirmus *(infirm)* 4.16; 27.6; 28.5; 31.9; 36.title, 1, 2, 4, 7, 8, 9, 10; 40.3; 42.4; 48.24; 64.19

invicem *(one another)* 22.6, 8; 35.1, 6; 54.1; 63.17; 65.8; 71.title, 1; 72.4

invidia *(envy)* 4.67; 65.7, 22

iubere *(to command)* 2.4; 5.8, 14; 31.5; 42.10; 44.4, 6, 8; 47.2, 4; 53.8; 54.3; 57.3; 60.4; 68.1

iudicare *(to judge)* 3.2, 5; 7.49; 18.22; 32.2; 43.7; 44.3; 62.8; 63.6; 65.14; 72.7

iudicium *(judgment)* 2.6, 9, 38; 3.11; 4.44, 76; 5.12; 7.64; 16.5; 24.2; 31.9; 55.22; 63.3; 64.10; 65.22

iustitia *(justice)* Prol. 25; 2.5, 9, 14, 19, 35; 4.33; 16.5; 73.title

iustus *(just)* 3.6; 41.5

to judge - iudicare

judgment - iudicium

just - iustus - - labor

justice - iustitia

to keep - conservare

to keep custody - custodire

king - rex

kingdom - regnum

labor Prol. 2; 7.68; 35.13; 39.6; 40.5; 41.2; 46.1; 48.1, 8, 24; 50.1

laborare *(to labor)* 46.1; 48.3, 11; 50.title; 64.18

lacrima *(tear)* 4.57; 20.3; 52.4

laudare *(to praise)* 11.8

laughter - risus

laus *(praise)* 9.1; 10.title; 11.10; 12.4; 13.11; 16.1, 3, 5; 38.3

lectio *(reading)* 4.55; 8.3; 9.5, 6, 9, 10; 10.2; 11.2; 11.4, 5, 7, 9, 12; 12.4; 13.11; 14.2

legere *(to read)* 9.5, 8; 10.2; 11.2, 5, 7, 9; 18.25; 38.1, 4, 5,10, 12; 40.6; 42.3, 4, 6; 47.3; 48.5, 15, 23; 53.9; 58.9, 2; 66.8

Lent - quadragesima

life - vita

light - lumen

light - lux

to live - vivere

loquacity - multiloquium

loqui *(speech)* Prol. 17, 26; 1.12; 4.52, 53; 6.3, 6; 7.56, 60; 26.1; 42.title; 42.8

loquacitas *(talkativeness)* 49.7

to love - amare

love - amor

love - dilectio

to love - diligere

loving - pius

lumen *(light)* Prol. 9, 13; 41.8

lux *(light)* Prol. 43; 8.4; 41.8, 9

magister *(master)* Prol. 1; 2.24; 3.6; 5.9; 6.6

mandatum *(commandment)* Prol. 49; 2.12; 7.54; 21.2; 26.1

measure - mensura

to measure - mensurare

medicamen *(medication)* 28.3

medicus *(physician)* 27.1, 2; 28.2

meminere *(to remember)* 2.1, 30, 35; 64.13

memor *(remembering)* 2.6, 26; 4.61; 7.11; 19.3; 31.8, 16

mensura *(measure)* 11.2; 24.1; 25.5; 30.1; 39.title; 40.title, 2,8; 49.6; 55.8; 68.2; 70.5

mensurare *(to measure)* 31.12; 48.9; 55.8

merciful - misericors

mercy - misericordia

militare *(fight)* Prol.3, 40; 1.2; 58.10; 61.10

militia *(the military)* 2.20

misericordia *(mercy)* 4.74; 7.46; 34.4; 37.1

misericors *(merciful)* 64.9

monasterium *(monastery)* Prol. 50; 1.3; 2.1, 16; 3.1, 8, 9, 12; 4.78; 7.55, 63; 21.title; 29.title, 1; 31.title, 1, 10, 12; 32.title, 1, 4; 33.1, 5; 48.17; 51.1; 52.title; 53.16, 19; 57.title, 1, 26; 58.15, 24, 26, 28, 29; 59.1, 4, 5; 60.title, 1, 6, 7, 8; 61.1, 2, 6, 13; 62.title, 5, 10; 63.1, 8; 65.title, 1, 11, 12, 21; 66.title,1, 6; 67.5, 7; 69.title, 1; 70.1; 71.9; 73.1

monastery - monasterium

mors *(death)* Prol. 13, 38, 50; 2.10, 29; 4.47; 6.5; 7.24, 34, 38; 57.5

multiloquium *(loquacity)* 6.4; 7.57; 20.3

murmurare *(to murmur)* 5.17, 18, 19; 23.1; 40.8

murmuratio *(murmuring)* 34.6; 35.13; 40.9; 41.5; 53.18

murmuriosus *(given to murmuring)* 4.39

murmurium *(murmuring)* 5.14

narrow - angustus

neglectus *(neglectful)* 11.13

neglegentia *(neglect)* 36.6; 43.14; 45.2; 49.3

neglegere *(to neglect)* 2.25; 7.22; 31.11; 32.4; 36.10; 43.5; 48.23; 50.4; 64.6; 73.7

oboedientia *(obedience)* Prol. 2, 3, 40; 2.6, 17; 5.title, 1, 8, 14, 15; 7.34, 35; 58.7, 17; 62.4; 68.1; 71.1, 2; 72. 6

oboedire *(to obey)* 2.25; 3.5, 6; 4.61; 5.5, 12, 17; 7.34; 53.20; 62.11; 65.21; 68.5; 71.title, 1, 4; 73.6

observantia *(observance)* Prol. 21, 29

observare *(to observe)* 7.18, 68; 58.10; 65.17; 73.1

observatio *(observance)* 3.11; 49.title, 1; 60.9; 73.title, 2

oculus *(eye)* Prol. 9, 18; 2.15; 4.47, 77; 7.3, 10, 26, 65; 19.1

officium *(office)* Prol. 39; 8.title; 16.2; 31.17; 35.1; 43.1; 47.3; 48.22; 53.3, 17, 19; 62.6

one another - invicem

to open wide - dilatare

opus *(work)* 1.7; 2.21; 4.title; 7.28, 63; 16.title; 19.2; 22.6, 8; 25.3; 27.1; 28.2; 41.4; 43.title, 3, 6, 10; 44.1, 7; 47.title, 1; 48.11, 23; 50.3; 52.2, 5; 53.18; 55.6, 16; 57.4; 58.7; 63.3; 67.2,3

orare *(to pray)* 4.72; 27.4; 35.15; 38.2; 43.13; 44.4; 52.3, 4; 58.23

oratio *(prayer)* Prol. 4, 56, 57; 7.20; 13.12, 13, 14; 17.5, 8; 20.title, 4, 5; 28.4; 49.4, 5, 8; 53.5, 8; 67.1, 2, 4

order - ordo

ordinare *(to ordain/appoint)* 18.22; 48.2; 60.1; 62.1, 2; 64.title, 2, 7; 65.3, 6, 12, 15

ordinatio *(ordination)* 60.6; 64.1; 65.1, 4, 11, 16

ordo *(order)* 2.19; 11.2, 4, 5, 7, 11; 13.12; 17.1, 5; 18.title, 5, 18, 20; 21.4; 38.12; 43.4, 5; 47.2; 48.15; 58.9; 60.1; 63.title, 1, 4, 5, 18; 64.2; 65.20

overindulgence - crapula

ovis *(sheep)* 2.7, 10, 39; 7.38; 27.5, 8; 28.8

Pascha *(Easter)* 8.1, 4; 10.1; 15.1, 4; 41.1, 7; 48.3; 49.7
pastor 1.8; 2.7, 8, 9, 39; 27.8
pater *(father)* Prol. 1, 6; 2.3, 24; 9.8; 31.2; 33.5; 42.3; 48.8; 49.9; 58.22; 73.2, 4, 5
patienter *(patiently)* 4.30; 36.5; 58.3; 68.2; 72.5
patientia *(patience)* Prol. 37, 50; 7.35, 42; 58.11
pauper 4.14; 31.9; 53.15; 55.9; 58.24; 59.title, 7; 66.3
paupertas *(poverty)* 48.7
pax *(peace)* Prol. 17; 4.25, 73; 34.5; 53.4, 5; 63.4; 65.11
peace - pax
peccator *(sinner)* Prol. 38; 7.65
peccatum *(sin)* 2.26, 28; 6.2, 4; 7.11,12, 57, 64, 70;46.5; 64.6
perfect - perfectus
perfectio *(perfection)* 73.2
perfectus *(perfect)* 5.9; 6.3; 7.67
perigrinus *(pilgrim)* 53.2, 15; 56.1; 61.title, 1
pervenire *(to persevere)* Prol. 22, 42; 7.5, 67; 63.19; 73.4, 9
petitio *(petition)* 58.3, 19, 20, 29; 59.1, 2, 3, 8
petition - petitio
physician - medicus
pilgrim - perigrinus
pius *(loving)* Prol 1, 38; 2,24; 7.30; 27.8; 37.3
poena *(punishment)* Prol. 7, 42; 2.10; 5.19; 6.2; 7.33
potestas *(power)* 39.6; 54.3; 56.2; 58.25; 63.2; 65.5; 70.2
poverty - paupertas
power - potestas
praeceptum *(precept)* Prol. 1, 39, 40; 2.4, 12; 4.61, 63; 7.42; 21.2; 23.1, 2; 54.1; 65.1; 70.6
praesumere *(to presume)* 3.4, 9, 10; 20.1; 26.1; 31.15; 33.2, 6; 38.8; 43.11,18; 44.6; 47.3; 51.1; 54.2, 5; 57.4; 60.5; 62.3, 8; 63.16; 67.5, 6, 7; 69.title, 1, 3; 70.title, 6
praesumptio *(presumption)* 49.9; 70.1
to praise - laudare
praise - laus
to pray - orare
prayer - oratio
precept - praeceptum

to presume - praesumere

presumption - praesumptio

pride - superbia

priest - sacerdos

priesthood - sacerdotium

prohibere *(to prohibit)* Prol.17; 7.19, 56; 31.15; 64.5

prosternere *(to prostrate)* 53.7; 58.23; 67.3; 71.8

proud - superbus

prudens *(prudent)* 61.4

psalmodia *(psalmody)* 10.1; 17.1; 18.20

psalterium *(psalter)* 8.3; 18.23, 24

punishment - poena

puritas *(purity)* 20.2, 3; 49.2

purus *(pure)* 20.4; 55.5; 63.11

Quadragesima (Lent) 15.2, 3; 41.6, 7; 48.10, 14, 15, 16; 49.title, 1, 2

ratio *(reason)* Prol. 47; 2.34, 37, 38; 3.11; 8.1; 24.4; 31.9; 63.3; 64.1, 7; 65.22; 70.5

to read - legere

reading - lectio

reason - ratio

to receive - accipere

to receive - suscipere

recitare *(to recite)* 9.10; 13.11; 17.4, 8; 24.4

to reflect/ponder - cogitare

regere *(to rule)* 2.31, 34, 37

regnum *(kingdom)* Prol.21, 22, 50; 2.35

regula *(rule)* 1.title, 2, 6; 3.7, 11; 7.55; 23.1; 37.1, 2; 42.9; 58.9, 12, 13, 15, 16; 60.2, 9; 62.4, 7, 11; 64.20; 65.17,18; 66.8; 73.title, 1, 5, 8

to remember - meminere

remembering - memor

to reserve time for - vacare

restraint in speech - taciturnitas

reverentia *(reverence)* 6.7; 9.7; 11.3; 20.title, 1; 52.2; 60.7; 63.12; 65.16

rex *(king)* Prol.3; 61.10

risus *(laughter)* 4.53, 54; 6.8; 7.59, 60

to rule - regere

rule - regula

to run - currere

sacerdos *(priest)* 60.title, 1; 61.12; 62.title, 8; 65.3

sacerdotium *(priesthood)* 60.7; 62.1, 4

to sadden - contristare

salus *(salvation, health)* Prol. 48; 2.33; 28.5

salvation, health - salus

sanctus *(holy)* Prol. 23, 35, 40; 1.9; 2.12; 4.55, 62; 5.3; 6.3; 7.70; 9.7; 14.title, 1; 15.1; 18.25; 21.1; 23.1; 38.10; 41.1; 49.3, 6, 7; 58.18, 19; 64.18; 65.18; 73.2, 4, 5

sanus *(sound, healthy)* 18.5; 27.1, 6; 35.10; 36.8; 44.6; 64.1

sapiens *(wise)* Prol. 33; 7.61; 19.4; 27.2; 28.2; 31.1; 40.7; 53.22; 66.1

sapientia *(wisdom)* 21.4; 64.2

satisfacere *(to satisfy)* 11.13; 43.12; 44.title, 3, 8, 9; 46.3; 71.8

satisfactio *(satisfaction)* 5.19; 24.4, 7; 27.3; 43.6, 11, 16; 44.8; 45.1

scandalizere *(to scandalize)* 31.16

scandalum *(scandal)* 65.1, 2; 69.3

scriptura *(scriptures)* Prol.8; 7.1, 19, 21, 25, 33, 36, 40, 45, 57; 28.3; 42.4

to see - videre

servare *(serve)* 1.7, 11; 2.23, 31; 18.10; 19.3; 35.1, 6, 13; 36.1, 4; 39.5, 10; 53.18; 58.14; 60.2; 61.10; 62.7

sheep - ovis

silentium *(silence)* 38.5; 42.1; 48.5; 52.2

sin - peccatum

to sing - canere

to sing/intone - cantare

sinner - peccator

to sleep - dormire

solacium *(solace)* 1.4; 31.17; 35.3, 4; 53.18, 20; 66.5

sollicitudo *(solicitude)* 2.33; 21.2; 27.1, 5; 31.9; 58.7; 71.4

sollicitus *(solicitous)* 2.39; 7.18; 22.3; 27.title; 36.7; 47.1; 53.15; 58.7; 65.17

son - filius

soul - anima

sound, healthy - sanus

vacare *(to reserve time for)* Prol. 43; 43.8; 48.13, 14, 17, 18, 23; 53.20

venire *(to come)* Prol. 12, 34; 1.13; 5.13; 7.32; 18.16; 44.4; 46.3; 53.6; 58.1, 3; 60.3; 63.8; 66.2

verbum *(word)* Prol. 33; 2.12, 27, 28; 4.53; 6.2, 8; 7.60, 61; 24.6; 34.6; 63.8; 65.18

via *(way)* Prol. 20, 24, 48, 49; 5.11; 6.1; 7.21, 45, 63; 50.title; 55.13, 14; 67.title, 1, 3, 4; 71.2

vice - vitium

videre *(to see)* Prol.15, 21; 2.15,19; 3.4; 4.42, 77; 7.13, 21,27,62; 17.1; 27.7; 28.4; 39.9; 43.5, 7; 48.18; 53.24; 57.2, 4; 58.3; 64.14; 65.11; 67.5; 68.2

virtue - virtus

virtus *(virtue)* 4.1; 7.69; 49.2; 64.19; 73.6, 9

vita *(life)* Prol. 13, 15, 17, 20, 36, 42, 43; 1.10; 4.46, 48; 5.3, 10, 11; 6.5; 7.5, 8, 11; 21.4; 32.1; 49.1, 2; 61.5, 12; 62.6; 63.1; 64.2; 72.2, 12; 73.3,

vitium *(vice)* Prol. 47; 1.5; 2.40; 7.12, 70; 13.13; 29.1; 33.1, 7; 43.14; 49.4; 55.18; 64.3, 4, 11, 14; 72.2

vivere *(to live)* Prol. 38; 5.12; 48.8; 58.21; 73.6, 7

vocare *(to call)* Prol. 21; 2.2; 3.3; 56.2; 63.12, 13

voice - vox

voluntas *(will)* Prol. 3; 1.11; 3.8; 4.60; 5.7, 13; 7.12, 19, 20, 21, 31, 32; 33.4; 49.6, 8, 10; 55.21; 61.5; 62.6; 65.16

vox *(voice)* Prol. 9, 10, 19; 5.8; 7.32, 59, 60; 19.7; 38.5, 7; 52.4

way - via
way of life - conversatio
weak/injured - debilis
will - voluntas
wisdom - sapientia
wise - sapiens
word - verbum
work - opus
worthy - dignus

zelus *(zeal)* 4.66; 64.6; 65.22; 72.title, 1, 2, 3